Optimizing Talent

*What Every Leader and Manager Needs
to Know to Sustain the Ultimate Workforce*

A volume in
Contemporary Trends in Organization Development and Change
Peter F. Sorensen and Therese F. Yaeger, *Series Editors*

What People Are Saying about Optimizing Talent

Good organizations spend a lot of time and effort trying to "manage talent," often with disappointing results. Sharkey and Eccher's excellent framework and examples will help you understand what organizations are doing wrong, and more importantly what you need to do to optimize talent and improve your organization's performance. This is a much-needed book!

—Jean-Francois Manzoni, PhD, Professor
IMD School of Business and author of *The Set-up to Fail Syndrome:
How Good Managers Cause Great People to Fail*

The Talent Optimization Framework™ provides thorough research and real-world recommendations for developing a talent-rich organization; this valuable book provides the reader with enduring wisdom.

—Jeanne K. Mason, Corporate Vice President Human Resources
Baxter International Inc.

This is a must read for leaders who want to get the most out of their talent equations and who believe their workforce is critical to their own success. Use it to assess what you are doing today and follow the advice to get the most out of your team.

—Mark Hutchinson, Vice President
General Electric Real Estate
GE International

As a CEO, I view the Talent Optimization Framework™ as a game changer for my organization and a much needed wake-up call for all of us who are fortunate enough to lead people; having used this framework, I have been able to dramatically improve the acquisition, assessment, development, and, ultimately, the performance of large commercial organizations.

—Paul J. Mirabella, Chairman & CEO
Naviscan, Inc.

Linda and Paul have brought real metrics and analytics to the development of talent in an organization. Every leader should have this book on their shelf!

—Art Harper, Founder, Managing Partner
GenNx360 Capital Partners

Sharkey and Eccher have put it all together in a highly constructive book that is not only thoroughly researched, but exquisitely written.

—Peter Sorenson, Jr., Ph.D.
Professor and Director of the Ph.D. program in Organization
Development (O.D.) and the M.S. program in Management and
Organizational Behavior at Benedictine University

Linda and Paul provide an easy-to-read, step-by-step approach to building talent. Most importantly they have provided the data and the analytics that prove the steps work.

—Nazneen Razi, Executive Vice President
and Chief Human Resources Officer
Jones Lang LaSalle, Inc.

The Talent Optimization Framework™ cuts through the talent management "noise" and delivers sound, practical advice on how to achieve bottom-line metrics through an integrated talent strategy.

—Kevin King, President and CEO
Affymetrix, Inc.

As the importance of talent grows so does the need to be systematic, data-based, and thoughtful about how you grow your talent. This book is full of pertinent, on-the-job examples and ways leaders can build talent in their teams and organizations.

—Jim Goodrich, Dean, School of Management
Alliant International University

The whole systems approach that Linda and Paul provide is ground breaking. Their Talent Optimization Framework™ is a proven tool to help you assess where you are relative to talent and build a clear strategy to achieve lasting results.

—Louis Carter, founder and CEO
Best Practice Institute

Contemporary Trends in Organization Development and Change

Peter F. Sorensen and Therese F. Yaeger, *Series Editors*

Global Organization Development: Managing Unprecedented Change
Edited by Therese F. Yaeger, Thomas C. Head, and Peter F. Sorensen

Strategic Organization Development: Managing Change for Success
Edited by Therese F. Yaeger and Peter F. Sorensen

Optimizing Talent

*What Every Leader and Manager Needs
to Know to Sustain the Ultimate Workforce*

Linda D. Sharkey, PhD
Paul H. Eccher, PhD

Foreword by Marshall Goldsmith

INFORMATION AGE PUBLISHING, INC.
Charlotte, NC • www.infoagepub.com

Library of Congress Cataloging-in-Publication Data

Sharkey, Linda.
  Optimizing talent : what every leader and manager needs to know to sustain the ultimate workforce / Linda D. Sharkey, Paul H. Eccher ; foreword by Marshall Goldsmith.
       p. cm. – (Contemporary trends in organization development and change)
  Includes bibliographical references.
  ISBN 978-1-61735-233-1 (pbk.) – ISBN 978-1-61735-234-8 (hbk.) – ISBN 978-1-61735-235-5 (e-book)
1. Manpower planning. 2. Human capital–Management. 3. Executive succession. 4. Employees–Training of. 5. Personnel management. I. Eccher, Paul H. II. Title.
  HF5549.5.M3S48 2010
  658.3'128–dc22
                                                                2010045148

Printed in the United States of America

Dedication

*To my husband Tom for all his love and support
and to my parents who would have been
so proud of this accomplishment*

*To my parents, Marino and Teresa, who provided me
with the belief in big dreams, and to my loving wife, Amy,
and beautiful girls, Gina and Mia, for their support,
wisdom, and humor that have made the pursuit
of big dreams such a wonderful journey.*

Contents

Preface

Optimizing Talent is a practical new book that offers down-to-earth advice and tools that are proven to work. The authors present a talent formula that ensures that talent practices align to business outcomes. What makes this book different from everything else out there is the real-life business experience, actionable advice, and fact-based evidence of what creates talent-rich organizations. The book is a call to action for managers and practitioners at all levels of organizations to make talent optimization a top priority every day!

The vast majority of organizations are searching for the "magic bullet" to improve talent. Research and experience drawn from extensive work with Fortune 500 companies have led Dr. Paul H. Eccher and Dr. Linda D. Sharkey to the conclusion that most organizations still come up dry in their attempts to develop a sustainable system—let alone one that allows for talent practices to be as well articulated and clear as most other operating mechanisms within companies.

The book provides an integrated framework for diagnosing talent optimization gaps. It demonstrates the improved business results achieved by organizations that excel at each lever in the framework. The work summarizes research conducted with over 500 companies and demonstrates which talent actions will drive integration and optimize talent. Dr. Sharkey and Dr. Eccher firmly believe that their work on the Talent Optimization Framework and Survey™ and the linkages between talent actions and organizational results provide the platform necessary to make talent optimization the top priority for every organization. They show that such tools and their appropriate use are critical to compete and win in today's business environment.

Business leaders, managers, talent practitioners, and scholars alike for whom this book is intended will learn to think strategically about people through the authors' insights into:

▪ Actions that allow sustainable business results to be garnered from improved talent management systems
▪ A Talent Optimization Framework™ (TOF) enabling an integrated approach to talent management and human capital
▪ Leveraging processes and tools to build talent for tangible results
▪ Establishing measures to achieve long-term improvement in talent capability
▪ Tools and strategies proven to enhance performance, reduce costs, and align processes
▪ The connection between a good talent system and a company's bottom line.

Each chapter falls into one of three sections—enabler, organization operating system, and results—and includes case studies, empirical data, and a checklist for action. Thus, readers can easily follow the authors through the process and implement similar programs, changes, or ideas at their own company. The importance of engaged leaders and a supportive culture are addressed, as is the value of a detailed organization operating system—comprised of the building blocks that will create the foundation for high-performance talent and the ability to measure meaningful results.

The hurdles of climbing into the talent management arena a challenger and climbing out a victor are many—but *Optimizing Talent* is an excellent coach to help you along your path to becoming the reigning champion.

Foreword

My purpose is to help successful people get even better. *Optimizing Talent: What Every Leader and Manager Needs to Know to Sustain the Ultimate Workforce* embodies this idea by helping organizations and their people improve. It is an essential book for leaders who want to create a legacy of a great organization, department, or team. It will expand your thinking about how you build talent and help you be more strategic about your talent, which is at the heart of every organization.

I first met Linda Sharkey when she was developing a coaching program for leaders at GE Capital. She asked me to help her to develop human resource talent to support and coach leaders using the Feed*Forward* techniques outlined in my book *What Got You Here Won't Get You There*. It was there that I saw Linda's passion for developing great leaders who focus on growing themselves, their people, and their teams.

Linda has continued this work over the years, and together with the incredible talent assessment and application expertise of Paul Eccher, developed methods at GE and HP that assess and provide actionable feedback to leaders. From the work of these two highly knowledgeable and experienced people, leaders have gained real insights into what they need more (and less) of as they move along their journeys of leadership.

What sets Paul and Linda apart from other "talent management experts" and puts such strength and power into their book is the research, science, and rigor they provide. They have a wealth of experience gained

Optimizing Talent, pages xiii–xiv
Copyright © 2011 by Information Age Publishing

through years of work with Fortune 500 companies, and both are hands-on practitioners as well as practical, serious researchers.

With the Talent Optimization Framework and Survey™, Linda and Paul have developed a whole-systems approach to talent management that helps companies "connect the dots" and achieve better bottom-line results. The framework is an interrelated set of building blocks that will help your organization become a talent-rich enterprise that is prepared for today's challenges as well as tomorrow's.

Whether you are a CEO, senior leader, team leader, or human resources professional, reading *Optimizing Talent: What Every Leader and Manager Needs to Know to Sustain the Ultimate Workforce* will help you breathe life into your talent practices and ensure that these practices yield significant, sustainable results!

Life is good.

—Marshall Goldsmith

World-renowned executive coach and author of the *New York Times* bestselling books, *Mojo: How to Get It, How to Keep It, How to Get It Back if You Lose It* (2010) and *What Got You Here Won't Get You There: How Successful People Become Even More Successful* (2007).

Acknowledgements

- A special thanks to Sarah McArthur our editor who guided us through this process with great expertise and calm. Her contribution to the book is immeasurable.
- To Kathy Hyatt Stewart for burning the midnight oil with Sarah to help get this book done with her great copy editing expertise.
- To Dave Ross, Co-Founder of The Vaya Group (formerly Corporate Insights) for providing sage advice and input that helped to shape our Talent Optimization Framework.
- To Mike Dulworth, CEO of Executive Networks, and the Executive Networks Team and members who helped us get our initial read on our survey, the power of the model and the concept and some of the insights and stories in the book.
- To Nick Isabella for wonderful artwork and a great cover for the book.
- To Benedictine University who taught us how to do research that makes a difference. Without our education and PhD's from Benedictine we could never have written this book.
- To the great team at The Vaya Group who gave us feedback on what we were doing and great help in analyzing data. Special thanks to Amy Eccher for her statistical analytics and data insights, to Amber Pye for all her great compelling charts, to Sandy "Sas" Ruffalo for her masterful proofing, and to Danita Eisenbise and Michelle Bush for their helpful ideas and suggestions along the way.

Optimizing Talent, pages xv–xvi
Copyright © 2011 by Information Age Publishing
All rights of reproduction in any form reserved.

- ▪ To Survey Connect who helped us with our on-line survey and data collection; thanks Marcie Levine, you did a great job.
- ▪ To the Marshall Goldsmith Group for their inspiration in writing books that make a difference and being a great team to be a part of.
- ▪ To Tripti Aggarwal for her great research on the top and bottom quartile companies.
- ▪ Lastly but not least of all to all the leaders and managers that we have worked with over the years that gave us the wealth of their experiences that makes this book so rich.

CHAPTER 1

GETTING STARTED

Optimizing Talent, pages 1–7
Copyright © 2011 by Information Age Publishing
All rights of reproduction in any form reserved.

Optimizing Talent is about the dramatic changes corporations must make in order to attract, develop, nurture, engage, and retain talented people—and why they must do so. At present, most companies treat talent as if it were a readily available commodity—similar to how US consumers have treated oil consumption for the past few generations. The practice has been to use it, waste it, and assume you can easily drill for more of it! As we've seen with oil, there is a limited supply.

In the pages of this book, we will explore why people in business have consistently ignored or behaved in manners that are the polar opposite of cultivating sustainable best-in-class talent pools. We've all seen people in leadership roles, to one degree or another, trying to take shortcuts in managing the talent in the organization. Some of us have even been those people using shortcuts. And if we were, we've been burned by the unintentional consequences of our actions.

Optimizing Talent is the call to action to everyone and anyone in a people leadership role to make talent management a key strategic business priority. Whether you are the president of a ten-billion-dollar multinational corporation, the human resources leader of a Fortune 1000 company, the leader of a nonprofit organization, or a small business leader with 30 employees, you will identify with the fact-based, rational case we make here for talent management, or what we call "talent optimization."

As business leaders, we are always on the lookout for solutions that will give our organizations and teams a competitive advantage. We seek to manage costs more efficiently, to reach more potential customers, to enhance quality of product, and to be admired as industry leaders. Over the past 25 years, one new cure-all after another has captured our attention and our wallets. Whether it's been Talent Quality Management (TQM), Six Sigma, lean manufacturing, advances in financial cost accounting, offshoring business operations, or the like, we have been eager to invest in the next great solution or "shortcut."

In the United States alone, corporations have invested billions of dollars in these solutions since 1990. Sometimes these investments pay great short-term dividends, but often the long-term results are disappointing. How could it be that so much capital is being invested in solutions that appear absolutely fail-safe on paper, but then disappoint in implementation? The answer is simple: people. Within this book, we will introduce you to the Talent Optimization Framework™ (TOF) and walk you through the key levers to pull in order to create an organization that sustains talent. By taking an integrated, data-based approach to talent, we will show how forward-looking companies are gaining financial and competitive advantages for themselves.

Up until now, when decisions regarding organization investments were being made, the sciences of finance, engineering, and quality management have been able to make clear and tangible arguments for how to decrease costs and, to some degree, increase revenues. The science of people and leadership has been less eloquent in making the case for investments in talent strategies.

Our argument is that the so-called "soft sciences" (psychology, organizational development, and human resources) must answer the call for greater rigor and data-based research in order to create a more balanced and sustainable look at how companies can reduce costs and increase revenues. Without this, we may find ourselves continuing down the track of

- Decreased employee loyalty and engagement
- Increased sense of workforce disenfranchisement and burnout
- Decreased innovation and breakthrough thinking
- Increased offshoring
- A leadership talent shortage

Talent Management

When did the notion of talent management emerge to become the buzzword of the day? It seems every book you pick up in the business literature has some angle around talent. Most are struggling for a clean definition of talent management. As we search the literature for a good definition, we see lots of corporate jargon. But leading companies have been focused on developing top talent for decades.

While business results have varied, GE, IBM, and GM, for instance, have a long history of focusing on their people (Cappelli, 2008). According to Cappelli, many companies used the military model from World War II and began actively looking at ways to identify, develop, and retain their leaders as the world of big business continued to expand after the war.

So why has the focus on talent management exploded in the business culture in the last five years? It may be because as companies globalize and expand, many realize that it is their talent that makes the difference. Without sharp talent, companies cannot move as quickly and nimbly to capture market share or anticipate the next-generation idea. Nor can they open new markets if they do not have the right talent to lead the initiative and engage the people on the front lines. Most corporate reports have a section on talent that highlights the effective leadership of the organization. And most stock valuations take into account the quality of the leadership talent as at least one factor in determining the viability of a company as a "hold, buy, or sell" (Dowd, 1992).

Leadership and talent do matter. They have always mattered, but again we ask, why the frenzy to develop them now? The burst of the technology bubble around the turn of the 21st century made the marketplace more competitive; markets became more liquid and global in reach, and time to market even more swift. "Disintermediation" (a term made popular by Christensen in 1997 [2003]) was swift and brutal. Products were here to-day and gone tomorrow or cloned quickly by others. The Amazon Kindle is a good example. It was not on the market for six months before three competing products equally as good became available. In fact, by the time this book is published, there will be many more Kindle-type devices in the marketplace.

One reason for the heightened focus on talent development of late is the valid fear that top talent can walk out the door to competitors easily (Michaels, 2001). This has changed a bit with the recent global economic crisis, during which many top people have held onto their positions as long as possible. But as the financial tide changes, so will the talent, and they will be looking to the exit once again. Another reason is that senior talent has their eye on retirement and there is a big gap between the senior-level expe-rience and the next level down (Erickson, 2008). Again, this has shifted due to the loss of some retirement plans in the recent economic downturn, but this will not stave off these retirements for long as more and more senior leaders prepare to leave the workplace.

Because of these well-documented dynamics, companies started invest-ing in their talent and began to focus on identifying top talent and how to retain them and keep their intellectual property. With turnover rates in Asia for most companies at around 22%–35%, retaining talent in these markets is and will continue to be exceedingly tough.

However, the recession has had a deep impact on this frenzy; compa-nies have been laying off at increased rates. Employees are working longer hours and extras have been cut to the bone to save money. The focus on people has taken a back seat to organizational survival and development activities have been curtailed or scrapped in efforts to save money. People have their heads down at work and articles are written daily about how to be a good employee in times of downturn. Employees are advised not to "rock the boat" and employers are hearing that this is a great time to "clean house" of people who aren't pulling their weight. People have nowhere to go, so businesses can retain them under any circumstances; they don't need to be concerned with engagement. Smart companies like PepsiCo, Cisco,

Walmart, and Genpact, however, never relinquish their efforts around talent development.

We expect this "recession reaction" to be short-lived as companies grapple with an improving economy and the fact that employee satisfaction surveys are at an all-time low (Gibbons, 2010). In fact, the questions asked on most surveys as key indicators of satisfaction are: "If you were offered another job of equal value would you leave?" and "Would you recommend this company as a good place for your friend to work?" Both of these questions have been validated as indicators of engagement and intent to stay with a current employer (Kaye and Jordan-Evans, 2008). The responses to these questions are lower than ever. There is a tremendous cynicism detected about leadership in the quantitative survey question responses; the qualitative responses are even more telling. The lack of trust in leaders by the average employee is extremely high.

Shockingly, this discontent appears to have crept into all levels of the organization. In the past, the higher you went up in an organization, the happier the talent was. These results have had a chilling effect on the C-suite and the boardrooms of large and small companies alike. We believe that this fact alone underscores the premise that talent is not only important, but the key differentiator for most successful companies.

If the above is true, and we believe as many do (Pink, 2009; Goldsmith, 2007b) that it is, what will be the most effective and efficient response to rebuild the talent focus in organizations? After researching the literature, attending conferences on "best practices," and reviewing company talent programs and initiatives, we know that no one has "cracked the code" on how to put a talent system that works in place at all levels of the organization. In particular, we have seen very little evidence of integrated talent development systems that yield top talent and strong business results. Also, there has been scarce connection and correlation between talent activities and longer-term business results.

According to Josh Bersin (2008), a leading researcher in the area of human resources, most talent initiatives are neither strategic nor integrated, and only about 5% of companies have a clear talent management strategy in place. Our experience, both working inside companies and consulting from outside, is that talent initiatives are often a "check-the-box" exercise not owned by the leadership, disconnected from the business strategy, and not yielding real bottom-line results. Therefore, we set out to discover how to develop a talent system that generates real advantage to the organization's bottom line and creates a culture of high performance and talent loyalty.

The first question we pondered was why talent *management?* Management infers something to be controlled, not necessarily something that is valued for the contribution it makes to the enterprise (Thorne and Pellant, 2007). As Thorne and Pellant rightly point out, the human equation should be about developing and helping talented people be the best they can no matter where they are in the organization, not just managing the process or "checking the box." Upon reflection, we decided that what was really at issue was companies being able to optimize the talent they had at all levels in order to maximize its contribution to the short- and long-term growth of the company. Thus we decided that this book should be about talent *optimization*, which goes beyond the idea of development or management. Optimization means that not only do you have to be clear about the development issues and opportunities; you also must have a culture that brings out the best in all members of the organization (Thorne and Pellant, 2007).

The other observation we made is that many defined human resources as the primary party for developing and retaining talent. While we agree that HR is a key element, it is not the *only* element.

Most important is the engagement of the leaders around talent. In the words of Jack Welch (Welch and Byrne, 2003), "You as leader must be the top human resource leader." Jack instilled this notion in the culture of GE, where even today leaders focus on their talent from hiring, developing, retaining, and promoting them. It is their badge of honor to "bring talent along." In fact, GE leaders take pride when others want to hire the talent they have groomed. They recognize that talent is central both to a leader's role and to an organization's strategy.

In response to the talent dilemma, we built the TOF, a model that is based on six simple principles that we will discuss in this book. It is an integrated and easy to follow whole-systems view that drives meaningful bottom-line results and is sustainable over time. This book lays out each component of our TOF and details why the component is important, how to assess your capability in each component, and what you can do to improve the components that are most important to your organization. Additionally, there are suggestions on how to make each component a "gold medal" winner. Finally, you will learn how to implement this model in your own organization whether you are a leader of a large or small, private or public enterprise or a human resources professional supporting a business. This is not an HR manual, but rather a book for all leaders who are trying to lead the most productive and high-performing organizations they can.

References

Bersin, J. (2008). *The training measurement book: Best practices, proven methodologies, and practical approaches.* San Francisco: Pfeiffer.

Cappelli, P. (2008). *Talent on demand: Managing talent in an age of uncertainty.* Boston: Harvard Business School Press.

Christensen, C. (2003). *The innovator's dilemma: The revolutionary book that will change the way you do business* (Rev. ed.). Boston: Harvard Business School Press.

Dowd, M. E. (1992). *Wall Street made simple.* Oxford, UK: Made Simple Books.

Erickson, T. (2008). *Retire: Career strategies for the boomer generation.* Boston: Harvard Business School Press.

Gibbons, J.M. (2010, January 5). I can't get no . . . job satisfaction, that is. *Conference Board Report* (R-1459-09-RR). New York: The Conference Board, Inc.

Goldsmith, M. (2007b). *What got you here won't get you there: How successful people become even more successful!* New York: Hyperion.

Kaye, B., & Jordan-Evans, S. (2008). *Love 'em or lose 'em: Getting good people to stay* (4th ed.). San Francisco: Berrett-Koehler Publishers.

Michaels, E. (2001). *The war for talent.* Boston: Harvard Business School Press.

Pink, D. (2009). *Drive: The surprising truth about what motivates us.* New York: Riverhead Books.

Thorne, K., & Pellant, A. (2007). *The essential guide to managing talent: How top companies recruit, train & retain the best employees.* London: Kogan Page.

Welch, J., & Byrne, J. A. (2003). *Jack: Straight from the gut.* New York: Business Plus.

CHAPTER 2

OVERVIEW
of the Talent Optimization Framework and Survey™

Optimizing Talent, pages 9–22
Copyright © 2011 by Information Age Publishing

9

Why is the talent equation so spotty? To answer this question, we first had to determine the root causes of why talent management efforts have been so ineffective. We found six basic undermining causes:

1. *Lack of Leadership Engagement:* Talent management efforts are born and reside within HR, and ownership and the ultimate success or failure of these efforts falls in the laps of the HR community. Without senior leader sponsorship and engagement, talent management initiatives often take on the look of programs versus critical organizational initiatives. When senior leaders do not engage in identifying and grooming talent in the organization, it sends a clear and crippling message to everyone in the company: "Don't worry, this talent management stuff just isn't very important to our business."

2. *No Clear Linkage between Business Strategy and Talent Management Strategy:* Too often companies start with the mechanics of a talent review process without fully defining what it is they are trying to accomplish. Without a clear understanding of the "why" or strategic intent of the effort, even with the best of intentions, the initiative feels reactionary and like a "check-the-box" exercise. To be successful, a clear articulation of how the talent management strategy supports business success in tangible, measurable terms is essential.

3. *Culture that Does Not Support Talent Initiatives:* We have found that leaders may be well intentioned about developing talent, but they do not see the underlying cultural elements that are impeding their efforts. Often leaders are more focused on results at the expense of people. Many are uncomfortable coaching talent and giving constructive feedback. Some don't believe in sharing talent. If the culture does not support development, invest in talent, and help people gain new experiences, then just about any talent initiative is doomed to die a quick death.

4. *No Overarching Framework:* For talent management efforts to be sustainable, there must be a common understanding and language for the enterprise relating to talent. It must be a clear and simple framework for showing how the important levers of talent management support the future success of the business. A consistent framework that has built-in flexibility (to account for business-unit differences) and unique regional priorities allows for local talent managers to formulate innovative solutions that are tailored to the respective unit's or region's needs. If units feel they can design their own plans with clear outcomes and accountabili-

ties, they are much more likely to drive the appropriate execution and change.

5. *Lack of an Integrated Approach:* According to Bersin and Associates, and in our experience, human resource processes can often be siloed. Additionally, alignment between the business strategy and these processes can be disconnected. This misalignment of activities costs money as the wrong talent is hired and/or development programs are not aligned to the most critical skill gaps. This causes considerable confusion about what is required of talent to get ahead.

6. *Lack of Transparency and Benchmarks for Assessing Results of Talent Management Initiatives:* Too often talent information is put in a black box never to see the light of day; even successes from the talent management initiative are not communicated. Some believe that talent management is a closed exercise, and therefore do not communicate the results openly and on a regular basis. People become cynical and don't see the results of the work and how actions taken are linked to the talent process, business strategy, and overall improvement of the company and its leaders. Transparent communication, specific goals, and clear metrics are critical and much overlooked aspects of talent management.

Our work with a Fortune 500 company illustrates how these six root causes often play out within organizations. One such scenario happened when the new HR leader was selected to create a "best-in-class" talent management initiative for the company. With grand enthusiasm and intentions, he leapt into action. Within a few short months, enthusiasm turned into worry and fear; progress was not going to be easy.

What happened? Our bright-eyed HR leader found he was unable to get the attention of those who had hired him. Senior leaders were immersed in a business crisis and had no time to dedicate to talent management initiatives. Undeterred, our HR leader plunged into creating a talent management strategy, but did so without any alignment or understanding of the business needs of the organization. The new talent management strategy was elaborate and necessitated peer-to-peer coaching and an aggressive approach to job assignment rotations. In attempting to roll out these ambitious plans, the fearless HR leader found that the company's culture was one in which peers competed with peers rather than coached them, and business leaders often hid their talent versus sharing or rotating them to new, enriching assignments. Tired and dejected, the HR leader reached out for answers. This is what he learned:

1. Engaging senior leaders is critical;
2. Align any talent management strategy to the business strategy;
3. Assess the culture before prescribing talent management solutions;
4. Rely on a clear talent management framework;
5. Recognize the critical levers to pull to succeed;
6. Measure, measure, and measure talent management outcomes with quantitative benchmarks.

Our Talent Management Framework™ (TOF) is based on these six principles and is simple, integrated, and easy to follow. It drives meaningful bottom-line results and is sustainable over time. Our model is patterned after the Malcolm Baldrige Model,[1] with inputs or key enablers, the system, and the results the system yields (see Figure 2.1). This model provides a framework for organizations that can be cascaded and repeated year after year to drive continued improvement. It should be embedded in the DNA of the company and be part of the strategic process that builds a talent optimization plan. No business would or could operate without a strong financial plan. Nor should it operate without a strong talent plan that is hardwired to the business strategy (Collins, 2009).

Survey questions for each aspect of the framework were developed to determine the quality of each aspect. The survey was then conducted globally with over 400 Fortune 1000 companies. The following sectors were included: retail, financial services, IT, manufacturing, insurance, hospital systems, and private not-for-profits. We then analyzed the data to see if the components of the framework would statistically hang together and if there were any critical correlations to bottom-line results. The results were astonishing. We believe that we have uncovered the hidden truths for how to develop a talent system that leads to high performance organizations.

Figure 2.1 The Talent Optimization Framework™.

---

1. For more about the Baldrige Model, please go to http://www.baldrige.com/

Building the Talent Optimization Framework™ (TOF)

Let's take a quick look at each component of the model (see Figure 2.2). These components will be explained in subsequent chapters of the book.

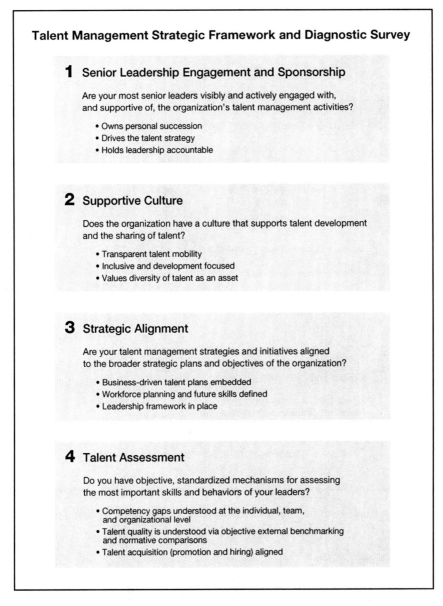

Talent Management Strategic Framework and Diagnostic Survey

1 Senior Leadership Engagement and Sponsorship

Are your most senior leaders visibly and actively engaged with, and supportive of, the organization's talent management activities?

- Owns personal succession
- Drives the talent strategy
- Holds leadership accountable

2 Supportive Culture

Does the organization have a culture that supports talent development and the sharing of talent?

- Transparent talent mobility
- Inclusive and development focused
- Values diversity of talent as an asset

3 Strategic Alignment

Are your talent management strategies and initiatives aligned to the broader strategic plans and objectives of the organization?

- Business-driven talent plans embedded
- Workforce planning and future skills defined
- Leadership framework in place

4 Talent Assessment

Do you have objective, standardized mechanisms for assessing the most important skills and behaviors of your leaders?

- Competency gaps understood at the individual, team, and organizational level
- Talent quality is understood via objective external benchmarking and normative comparisons
- Talent acquisition (promotion and hiring) aligned

Figure 2.2 Components of the Talent Optimization Framework and Survey™.

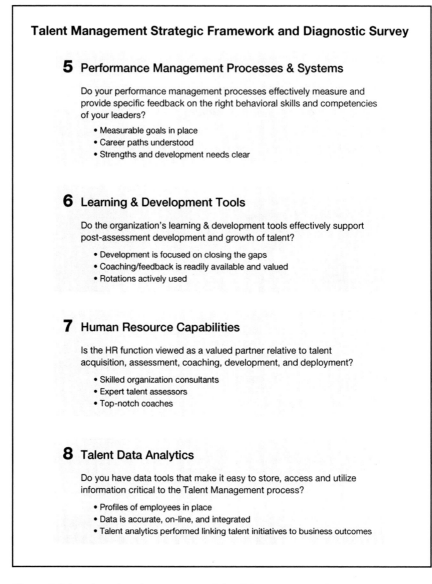

Talent Management Strategic Framework and Diagnostic Survey

5 Performance Management Processes & Systems

Do your performance management processes effectively measure and provide specific feedback on the right behavioral skills and competencies of your leaders?

- Measurable goals in place
- Career paths understood
- Strengths and development needs clear

6 Learning & Development Tools

Do the organization's learning & development tools effectively support post-assessment development and growth of talent?

- Development is focused on closing the gaps
- Coaching/feedback is readily available and valued
- Rotations actively used

7 Human Resource Capabilities

Is the HR function viewed as a valued partner relative to talent acquisition, assessment, coaching, development, and deployment?

- Skilled organization consultants
- Expert talent assessors
- Top-notch coaches

8 Talent Data Analytics

Do you have data tools that make it easy to store, access and utilize information critical to the Talent Management process?

- Profiles of employees in place
- Data is accurate, on-line, and integrated
- Talent analytics performed linking talent initiatives to business outcomes

Figure 2.2 (continued) Components of the Talent Optimization Framework and Survey™.

Leadership Engagement: Refers to the commitment and visibility of the most senior leaders (the C-suite and their direct reports) in the organization to talent initiatives. Specifically, are they personally involved in talent activities and do they communicate their support in their daily actions?

Supportive Culture: Means that the values of the organization are clear and explicitly support talent and people development. Leaders act consistently with those values, and the processes and rewards in place align to the values.

Strategic Alignment: Simply put, this refers to ensuring that your business strategy has been analyzed for talent requirements. A talent strategy is developed and used that supports the business imperatives.

Talent Assessment: Requires that leadership competencies that support the business strategy are explicitly defined. These competencies are then systematically assessed to determine strengths and gaps.

Performance Management Processes and Systems: Is a system that underscores not only the performance of the individual against business goals, but also includes personal development needs and career aspirations. The system is directly linked to the business strategy and talent assessment feedback.

Learning and Development: There are well-thought-out learning strategies in place to keep talented people at the top of their game and to close the development gaps defined through talent assessments.

Human Resource Capability: Refers to the ability of your human resource department to play a strategic role in coaching and assessing talent. It also includes the department's ability to assess culture, develop strategic interventions, and use data to show results that are tied to business outcomes.

Talent Data Analytics: Means having the correct data that are accessible and usable for talent decision making. Additionally, the data are analyzed to gain insights into talent actions and their impact on business performance.

Results: Refers to the actual outcomes that an organization derives from being strategic about its talent initiatives. It includes such items as retention, employee engagement, customer satisfaction, employee diversity, and better market place performance.

After decades of experience working with large corporations, HR organizations, and individual executives, directors, and managers, it became abundantly clear that most of us didn't have much of a clue how to optimize talent. Client organizations tended to fixate on short-term fixes to talent issues. Working with organizations, we heard things like

- "We need to develop our leadership pipeline, and we need you to assess and give coaching feedback to our top 200 high-potential leaders."

- "We keep hiring leaders who look great on paper, perfect background and pedigree, but so many of them turn over within the first 18 months!"
- "We want a meritocracy. Can you help us revamp our performance management system?"
- "We need our HR managers to be better equipped as business partners and executive coaches to their business leaders. Can you train them in these areas?"

All of these requests are reasonable and logical. So what is the problem? The problem is that all too often we tackle symptoms of a broken talent strategy without ever recognizing it as broken. Instead, organizations, consultants, and managers look for the quick siloed fix around talent. They go down a path that is unlikely to yield sustainable results or to build a data-based, measurable platform that will make the case for increased attention and funding for talent initiatives. These reactive, tactical approaches enter organizations like fads and then fade away quickly. Without a strategic and systematic framework for talent sustainability, researchers, practitioners, executives, and managers have little chance of changing the game on talent within an organization.

The irony is that business schools have taught us that it is nonsensical to attempt to build a thriving business without a clear vision and strategy. However, when we look to the people side of the equation, we often approach strategic issues as if we were medical nurses in a MASH unit, moving swiftly to "Band-Aid" damage rather than addressing the cause of the injury.

Why Begin with a Framework?

The lessons learned in implementing talent systems in large companies are clear. Headquarters (HQ) is always accused of dreaming up work for the field and the field is often viewed by HQ as playing "rogue" and doing their own thing. The mantra is that HQ does not understand what people in the field deal with and vice versa.

Even when there is collaboration between parties, there still seems to be tension between the groups that is counterproductive. People in the field often want to be creative, designing initiatives that meet their local needs. However, the HQ centers of excellence (COEs) often see this creativity as additional cost or duplication and so they work to standardize the processes across the organization. Standardization at some level is good and essential, but anything used to an excess is not so good. Having seen organizations with no standardization, we've found it causes confusion about what is expected and provides no consistency from a business-wide perspective. There is no synergy between the sum and its parts. On the other hand, organizations that are too standardized and inflexible leave no room for adapting to changing circumstances and requirements.

The truth of the matter is that one size does not fit all. A framework provides criteria within which everyone can work. It creates a common language and understanding of what is important, but it also allows both the field and HQ to respond appropriately to the specific conditions that exist in different businesses, regions, or levels of the organization.

A framework establishes a common lens with which to take action. It allows the organization as a whole to see what the greatest common gaps are and design "interventions" that will close those gaps company-wide, reducing duplication. Local parts of the company can design strategies that best fit their unique circumstances to close their gaps.

It was our hypothesis that many of the activities around talent initiatives were tactical in nature. The real enablers for change were leadership and the hidden aspects of the culture that would promote or inhibit any tactic or strategy from being implemented.

We set out to identify the most powerful components that align with talent optimization and bottom-line results. We also suspected that some aspects of company talent systems, in addition to leadership and culture, were more important than others in driving sustainable results.

In our research, discussions with talent leaders, and experiences, we were surprised to find so few integrated approaches to talent management. Most of the activities were siloed and did not provide a "whole systems" view to talent. From an analytical perspective, we found very little that tied talent activities to bottom-line results.

We wanted to provide an integrated talent model that could link to bottom-line results, which is why we designed a framework that starts with the enablers of leadership and culture and then looks at all the critical elements of the organization from a human capital point of view. Finally, we identified and defined the critical and tangible business outcomes associated with talent systems, including:

- Low turnover rate among high performers
- Increased employee engagement
- Improved diversity of talent
- Increased customer satisfaction
- Better market performance

We believe that there is not enough rigor in the human capital approaches that organizations use. Actions are not measured against bottom-line results. Most companies use disciplined analytics when it comes to marketing, testing customer attitudes, and determining what will bring a customer back for repeat business, but little effort is made to use similar approaches for the talent in organizations. Much is written about engagement (Kaye & Jordan-Evans, 2008), but a whole system does not exist where talent is analyzed, segmented, and developed based upon solid employee data that is known to ensure high performance and retention.

Components of the Talent Optimization Framework™ (TOF)

Each aspect of the TOF is an important piece of the talent puzzle. While some levers are more highly correlated to results than others, they all play an important, integrated role in creating a winning talent strategy (see Figure 2.3).

The results in Figure 2.3 show that organizations must have a supportive culture, strategic alignment, and learning and development processes in place if they are to optimize talent. Not only are these the hardest elements to address, but they are also the least worked on by talent professionals. Too often, we found that this was not because they did not want to, but because organization dynamics did not allow it.

We wondered if this could be a cultural issue. When we initially ran the survey with companies with revenue over $30 billion, we discovered an

RANKED HIGH TO LOW	TALENT OPTIMIZATION FRAMEWORK RESULTS
1 Supportive Culture	.77
2 Strategic Alignment	.76
3 Learning and Development	.69
4 Senior Leadership Engagement and Sponsorship	.68
5 Talent Assessment	.68
6 Human Resources Capabilities	.66
7 Talent Data Analytics	.66
8 Performance Management Processes and Systems	.53

Figure 2.3   Correlation analysis TOF levers relationship with TOF results.

interesting, but not surprising, fact. The talent levers that were more tactical in nature and part of the operating system, such as performance management, succession planning, talent reviews, data collection, and training, were rated highest; however, the more strategic and cultural aspects were much less developed. As you will see in chapter 3, these trends continued in the larger sample we surveyed.

In a dialogue with key talent leaders from the initial survey group, the observation was made that, "We have been told by the experts that we need to be more data-driven and more focused on strategic implementation, but the results of our own assessment show we are still missing the mark." Boudreau and Ramstad (2007) would support this observation about how human resources spend their time. Those of us who work in the field are not surprised with the results.

Table 2.1 shows how the elements of the TOF were ranked in importance from a statistical perspective versus where the talent professionals rated the quality of what they had in their talent systems. The disconnect is clear. As you can see, the most important lever, Supportive Culture, is where talent professionals spend almost the least amount of their time (only Talent Data Analytics came in lower). Conversely, talent professionals spend the greatest amount of time in Performance Management Processes and Systems, which is the least impactful lever.

Consistently, every organization had a defined talent review process using some method of determining performance versus potential. Most had a succession planning process in place. Most did talent reviews at the top

TABLE 2.1 Talent Optimization Framework™ (TOF)—Comparison of Highest Rated Levers and Most Important Levers

Most Important Levers	Elements of the Talent Optimization Framework™ (TOF)	Where Talent Professionals Spend their Time
1	Supportive Culture	7
2	Strategic Alignment	4
3	Learning and Development	2
4	Senior Leadership Engagement	5
5	Talent Assessment	6
6	Human Resources Capability	3
7	Talent Data Analytics	8
8	Performance Management Processes and Systems	1

of the house with very few going deeper in their management ranks. What was startling was the lack of tangible results from these processes. Very few companies cited that they filled open positions from the succession plans or used the data in their hiring and replacement strategies. They were much more reactionary when a job became open.

So, why spend all this time doing talent reviews if the data are not used to feed development promotions, recruitment needs, performance assessments, career planning, and the like?

During interviews, a leader told us that his organization started talent reviews at 6:00 a.m. and did not conclude until midnight the next evening; this was only for one business unit! He said this went on for at least a month. Another company that started reviews in January was not finished until five months later. By the time they were over, everyone was "brain-dead."

We are not saying that this level of assessment is unimportant: our analysis indicates that it is. However, what we are not seeing are the data derived from these sessions being used in any meaningful way. Another interesting finding of our research is that compensation is relatively neutral in driving real business results. We are not minimizing the importance of fair compensation, but we found that it is not a key lever for long-term results. Our findings bear out what is already known about compensation. It must be fair to the market. If you are substantially underpaying, the effect is dramatic in terms of retention in tight labor markets, but overpaying does not yield any substantial improvement in the performance of the company. It merely retains people for a short period of time until something better comes along. People need to be motivated for the longer term, and, as Daniel Pink (2009) has demonstrated, there are elements that are much more important than compensation, e.g., culture, yet most companies focus on compensation more than culture.

Having a culture where people feel valued is another significant factor that emerged from our study. Again, this is not surprising as employee satisfaction results have been at an all-time low (Gibbons, 2010). The cultural and leadership elements tended to blend together in the survey results. That is because it is difficult to separate what leaders do from what the culture actually is.

We know conclusively that what leaders do is a direct outgrowth of what they value and these values drive the essence of a company culture (Cooke, 1997). In our research, it was important that leaders were visible, that they coached their employees, and that the company was branded as a place for developing great leaders. Having these elements in play in an organization showed strong correlation to results, particularly retention, engagement, and diversity.

Symptoms of a Broken Talent System

We have seen these symptoms consistently throughout our work. Take a look at this list. Do you recognize yourself or your organization in any of these descriptions?

- Saying one thing and doing the opposite
- Rewarding destructive employees who get short-term results at all cost
- Assessing employees, expecting behavioral improvement, but providing no opportunities for development
- Overloading training modules with too much content or content that most employees can't readily practice in their jobs
- Hiding and holding back high-potential employees so that you don't lose them
- Making performance reviews a once-a-year event (that can be completed via email with no supervisor-employee dialogue)
- Building a culture in which taking time to learn and seeking advice on how to improve is frowned upon and interpreted as a sign of weakness
- Telling HR managers to coach and develop employees, while burying them with administrative work and providing them with no coaching training
- Creating environments in which employees feel like replaceable parts that are employed only until a cheaper solution is found
- Proclaiming that talent development is a nice thing to do, but first and foremost the company must focus on hitting its goals and financial metrics.

In the remainder of the book, we will take you through the details of our findings. We will also discuss each of the eight levers of the TOF to provide a deeper understanding of what must be done to fully leverage and integrate each lever into a sustainable talent advantage. We conclude with a quick quiz to help you assess where you stand relative to talent optimization and offer some tips and best practices to help you raise your game.

References

Boudreau, J.W., & Ramstad, P. M. (2007). *Beyond HR: The new science of human capital.* Boston: Harvard Business School Press.

Collins, J. (2009). *How the mighty fall: And why some companies never give in.* Self-published.

Cooke, R. A. (1997). *Leadership/Impact feedback report.* Plymouth, MI: Human Synergistics International.

Gibbons, J.M. (2010, January 5). I can't get no . . . job satisfaction, that is. *Conference Board Report* (R-1459-09-RR). New York: The Conference Board, Inc.

Kaye, B., & Jordan-Evans, S. (2008). *Love 'em or lose 'em: Getting good people to stay* (4th ed.). San Francisco: Berrett-Koehler Publishers.

Pink, D. (2009). *Drive: The surprising truth about what motivates us.* New York: Riverhead Books.

CHAPTER 3

OPTIMIZING THE TALENT POOL

Results and Findings

Optimizing Talent, pages 23–37

When we set out to "crack the code" on the key levers that support and sustain talent optimization, we quickly recognized that a logical, integrated model like the Talent Optimization Framework™ (TOF) was a necessary first step. We knew that we needed to account for the key components that can either be talent gainers or drainers for organizations, as well as show the interdependencies between the different talent levers.

We were gratified and reinforced by the comments and feedback we received regarding the framework. Our colleagues and clients viewed the TOF as "spot on" and an excellent way to better understand what to do in order to optimize talent in their organizations. "Hooray for the TOF! Hooray for us!" We could have said. However, we knew that in the grand scheme of things, creating the framework was the easy part. Validating the framework through research and data analytics was by far the more challenging and important aspect of our work

To generate the data necessary to put the TOF to the test of analytics, we constructed a survey instrument to assess each aspect of the framework as well as to collect data regarding the business outcomes achieved by the study of participants' organizations. Additionally, we looked at third-party, business-outcome data sources to further investigate the relationships between talent practices and business results. We examined the relationship between TOF results and historical stock price, as well as between TOF results and rankings in the following three company designations:

1. Best Places to Work Rankings
2. Most Admired Company Rankings
3. World's Most Sustainable Company Rankings

Our hypotheses were as follows:

1. Few companies will demonstrate consistent strengths across the integrated TOF.
2. Organizations showing greater strengths across the framework will also demonstrate stronger results on business-outcome measures.
3. The framework enablers of supportive culture and leadership coupled with effective strategic alignment will be highly correlated with positive business outcomes.
4. Corporations with stronger results on the TOF will demonstrate better stock price movement and receive higher rankings on external measures of quality.

Talent Optimization Framework™ (TOF): The Current State

In our study of over 400 organizations, we found a mixed bag of results regarding how organizations were performing on each of the talent levers. As noted in chapter 2, the lever that was viewed as most effective by respondents was performance management, with strategic alignment coming in last. The percentages of respondents reporting that their organizations were either effective or very effective on each TOF lever are displayed in Figure 3.1.

The response patterns from most of the organizations indicated that there were some positive activities occurring in each area; however, less than one in five organizations scored consistently well across the framework by demonstrating balanced strengths across all levers. The findings also support the notion that most organizations were not focusing enough attention on their key talent enablers (leadership and culture); as well as strategic alignment, talent assessment, and data analytics. We will see later in this chapter how even slight increases in these key areas can increase organizational results.

To further investigate how effective organizations were in terms of their TOF results, we examined the specific practices that were viewed as effective versus ineffective.

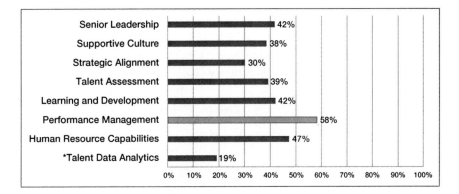

Figure 3.1 Percentages of respondents reporting that their organizations were either effective or very effective.

* While most organizations gave average ratings to data storage, few viewed their data analytics practices as being sufficient. This significantly pulled scores down in this category.

Highest Rated Talent Optimization Framework™ Items

- There is a regular and consistent performance review process in place that is used throughout the organization. It is easily understood, repeatable, reliable, and measurable.
- Employees have access to information relative to open positions within the organization for which they can apply.
- The performance review process provides consistent and candid feedback to employees regarding performance results, behaviors, and development needs.
- Rewards and compensation are directly tied to performance outcomes, including expected behaviors.
- Senior leaders regularly participate in talent reviews and move talent based upon business needs and personal aspirations of the talent.
- There is a specific framework for leadership competency requirements linked to business requirements and articulated in behavioral terms.
- Human resources is a key architect in the development process through the entire employee life cycle.
- Leaders and managers are held accountable for the ratings they provide in the performance review process (e.g., must justify them to others in calibration meetings).
- Rating levels included in the talent review and performance appraisal processes are detailed and specific enough to ensure calibration across all users.

The vast majority of items scoring well focused upon the performance management processes within organizations.

Lowest Rated Talent Optimization Framework™ Items

- Leadership development and career advancement paths have been created for different levels of leadership potential as opposed to being solely focused on top talent.
- The organization tracks the percentage of high potentials who make upward career moves.
- Robust succession plans exist and are used to fill positions throughout the executive ranks.
- The talent management vision and strategy clearly define the current and future (three to five years) talent needs of the organization and the knowledge, skills, and abilities most critical to short- and long-term success.

- The talent strategy has clear measures in place that are regularly tracked and reviewed.
- Talent management strategies account for market changes as well as the talent management strategies of competitors.
- An information management system is used to store talent information that is available to all managers and regularly updated.
- The organization uses external benchmarking and norm comparisons to calibrate quality of leadership talent.
- The talent information management system connects the key elements relative to people (promotions, compensation, performance, leadership strength and development needs, technical competency, etc.).
- The talent information management system is used regularly to make decisions about talent and overall organization people capability.
- Talent management data trends are analyzed and the data are used to improve upon talent management strategies for the business.
- ROI studies are conducted to assess the impact and leadership improvement associated with major leadership development initiatives.
- Analytical models are used for assessing the impact of human capital practices on organizational performance.

Contrast these low-ranking items with those that scored the highest. We see weaknesses in the areas of strategic alignment, talent assessment, learning and development, and data analytics. The data indicate that most organizations were struggling to develop a clear talent strategy for themselves and were woeful in their methods for analyzing talent data to better understand what was and was not working. Since these are the areas that directly influence results, these key levers provide opportunities to focus upon in order to positively impact the talent equation of an organization.

Overall, the results indicated that about one in five organizations appeared to have a balanced set of strengths across the TOF. It is encouraging to know that there are companies serving as good role models for talent optimization. Conversely, approximately one in four organizations displayed low scores on the TOF. These organizations tended to focus their efforts on creating a clear process and cadence for their performance review initiatives, but often to the exclusion of taking actions and organizational alignment for their talent approaches.

Linking Effectiveness to Business Outcomes with the Talent Optimization Framework™

The next aspect we looked at was the relationships between each of the talent levers and the outcome measures. Here, we began to explore the "so what?" behind the TOF. We wanted to better understand how organizations' TOF scores correlated with relevant measures of business performance. The following outcome measures were utilized to get a clear read on how well organizations have performed over the last 12 months:

- ▪ Business results consistently surpass those of market competitors.
- ▪ Employee satisfaction survey results display improvement in the areas of engagement, performance feedback, and development.
- ▪ Retention of high-potential leaders has increased.
- ▪ Diverse promotions have increased at the leadership level.

To better understand this relationship, we correlated the results of the TOF for each organization studied with the business-outcome items contained at the end of the survey instrument (see Figure 3.2).

This analysis displays strong correlations between each of the talent levers and business outcome measures. In this analysis, supportive culture surfaces as the lever that is most correlated with overall positive outcomes. While you may be a bit surprised (as were we) that leadership isn't the strongest correlation, we did find that leadership is the dominant driver of culture and strategy. This suggests that an organization wanting to positively impact its talent optimization must place a priority on understanding and shaping a supportive talent culture. While supportive culture tends to be the single best predictor of talent optimization, our results found this area to be one of the lowest scored. In most of the organizations we studied, the data tell us that not enough is being done to create environments that support talent optimization.

Other talent levers that demonstrated strong positive correlations to overall business outcomes were strategic alignment and talent assessment, with learning and development close behind. Another insight that emerged from the data is the connection between talent assessment and learning and development. We found that a precursor to having top-notch learning and development results was having a highly effective protocol for the assessment of talent. It appears that having reliable and rich data regarding the strengths and development opportunities of leaders at each level of the organization provides the insights and directions for creating a learning and development strategy that is aligned to the unique needs of the organization.

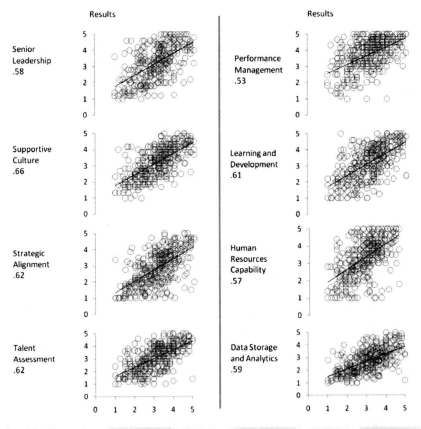

RELATIONSHIP BETWEEN LEVERS AND RESULTS	Results–The Best Talent, Increased Diversity of Talent, Lower Cost, Improved Business Outcomes	Business Units' Results Consistently Surpass the Market Competitors over the Last 12 Months	Employee Survey Results Display Improvement in the Areas of Engagement, Performance Feedback, and Development	Retention of High-Potential Leaders Has Increased over the Last 12 Months	Diverse Promotions Have Increased at the Leadership Level over the Last 12 Months
Senior Leadership Engagement and Sponsorship	.58	.44	.52	.36	.44
Supportive Culture	.66	.49	.51	.45	.52
Strategic Alignment	.62	.42	.55	.37	.49
Talent Assessment	.62	.45	.55	.37	.44
Performance Management Processes and Systems	.53	.41	.48	.40	.39
Learning and Development	.61	.44	.57	.36	.44
Human Resources Capabilities	.57	.52	.42	.48	.43
Talent Data Analytics	.59	.35	.53	.36	.48

All correlations significant at 99% confidence level

Figure 3.2

Next, we explored whether there were different talent levers that could be considered "drivers" of each of the outcome measures utilized. When we look at the individual outcome measures, it appears that organizations demonstrating strengths in most or all TOF levers are much more likely to have a highly engaged, developmentally focused workforce. Conversely, 90% of the organizations that scored low on the TOF also scored low (bottom two quartiles) on business results (see Figure 3.3).

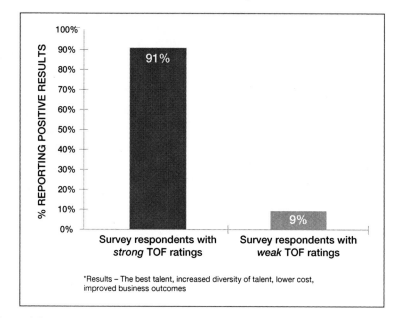

Figure 3.3

When we honed in on the drivers of positive business unit results, the TOF levers of HR capabilities, supportive culture, and talent assessment were most dominant. One more interesting finding was that organizations that were excelling at increasing diversity had strong supportive cultures, excellent strategic alignment, and superb data analytics. This finding suggests that the central pillars for fostering a diverse talent pool are to create an environment that values diversity of thought and style, to have a talent strategy for increasing diversity, and lastly, to regularly assess progress on talent plans.

Another way to illustrate the strong relationship between TOF practices and business outcomes can be seen in Figure 3.4. We compared business outcomes for organizations scoring at the top quartile with those in the bottom quartile. The TOF gaps between these two groups are quite telling. The top quartile group demonstrates high scores on TOF practices, while the bottom quartile group hovers in the marginally effective to low range in most areas.

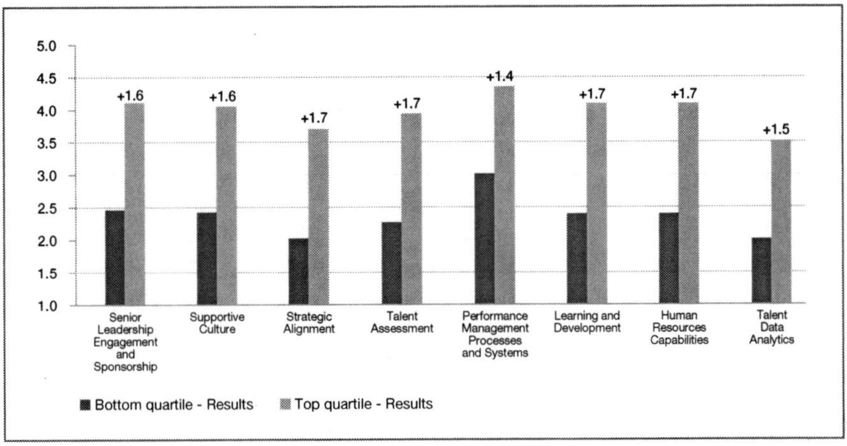

Figure 3.4

On an individual item basis, the correlations we found suggest a strong relationship of TOF practices to business outcomes; in fact, it was telling that all of the individual items had a significant and solid relationship with organizational results. The specific items that were the strongest drivers of positive business outcomes are listed below. These items will be the cornerstone for building a model that will shed light on the predictive power and interaction of the TOF levers.

Items that Most Influence Overall Business Outcomes

- Succession plans are used regularly to fill key roles;
- Learning and development interventions allow for follow-up measures of the positive impact of the intervention;
- Learning, experimentation, seeking feedback, and mentoring colleagues are all evident within the organization;
- Talent gaps are understood at the individual, team, and organization level and measurable plans are in place to close these gaps;
- There is a well-articulated talent management vision and strategy aligned with the business requirements/priorities;
- Talent management strategies account for market changes as well as the talent management strategies of competitors.

In terms of the connection between TOF items and each specific results item, we see strong correlations and consistent themes. The items most correlated with each of the four key business outcomes identified earlier can be found in Table 3.1.

So how much does the TOF help us account for and drive positive business outcomes? After investigating item by item, lever by lever, how do all of these measures work together to predict organizational results? To answer this question, we conducted a linear regression analysis to explore how much of the business outcome's piece of the pie can be explained by the TOF levers (see Figure 3.5).

The correlations that we have already discussed suggested that the predictive model would yield strong results. Think of the many variables that can impact business outcomes, such as social and economic issues, organizational demographics, and the TOF levers. The TOF model accounts for 55% of the variation in business outcomes.

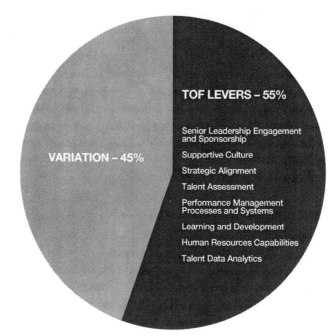

Figure 3.5

As Figure 3.5 illustrates, over 50% of the variance in business outcomes can be accounted for by the TOF levers. This provides substantial evidence in support of the validity of the model as a driver of positive business outcomes. This analysis also allowed us to examine the interplay between different levers in the model. We were able to build a statistical tool that can project the expected improvement in outcomes based on improving effec-

TABLE 3.1 Items Correlated with Four Key Business Outcomes

Items with the Greatest Influence on Business Results Surpassing Those of Market Competitors	Items with the Greatest Influence on Employee Engagement, Performance Feedback, and Development	Items with the Greatest Influence on Retention of High-Potential Leaders	Items with the Greatest Influence on Diverse Promotions
• Human resources is a key architect in the development process through the entire employee life cycle • Human resources professionals are expert talent assessors and provide career counseling to employees • Human resources professionals are seen as expert organization consultants relative to talent identification, development, and cultural change • Learning, experimentation, seeking feedback, and mentoring colleagues are all evident within the organization • The talent management vision and strategy clearly define the current and future (three to five years) talent needs of the organization and the knowledge, skills, and abilities most critical to short- and long-term success	• There is a well-articulated talent management vision and strategy aligned with the business requirements/priorities • Talent gaps are understood at the individual, team, and organization level and measurable plans are in place to close the gaps • There is a specific framework for leadership competency requirements linked to business requirements and articulated in behavioral terms • The organization tracks the percentage of high-potentials who make upward career moves • Learning and development makes use of multiple methods to accommodate diverse learning styles (job assignments, coaches, mentors, classroom training, etc.)	• Human resources professionals are expert talent assessors and provide career counseling to employees • Human resources professionals are seen as expert organization consultants relative to talent identification, development, and cultural change • Human resources is a key architect in the development process through the entire employee life cycle • Human resources professionals are skilled coaches to senior leaders in the organization • Learning, experimentation, seeking feedback, and mentoring colleagues are all evident within the organization	• Learning and development interventions allow for follow-up measure of the positive impact of the intervention • Succession plans are used regularly to fill key roles • There is a well-articulated talent management vision and strategy aligned with the business requirements/priorities • The talent management vision and strategy clearly define the current and future (three to five years) talent needs of the organization and the knowledge, skills, and abilities most critical to short- and long-term success • Senior leaders communicate regularly and send consistent messages in support of talent management and leadership development initiatives • Talent management strategies account for market changes as well as the talent management strategies of competitors • Analytical models are used for assessing the impact of human capital practices on organizational performance

tiveness on a particular talent lever. This can be a very useful tool to utilize when determining where to best invest scarce resources in order to get the "biggest bang for your buck" in business outcomes.

Let's start with an organization with average scores across the levers. The predicted results score is average. What we can show from this model is that even a one-point increase, which is a doable increase for an average organization, can impact results more if the increase is in the supportive culture and strategic alignment areas as opposed to the performance management processes and systems area (see Figure 3.6).

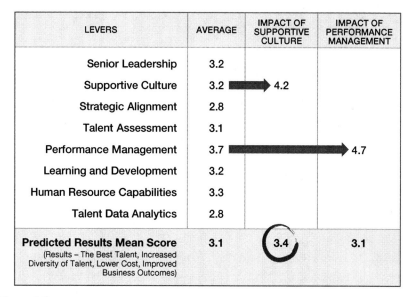

LEVERS	AVERAGE	IMPACT OF SUPPORTIVE CULTURE	IMPACT OF PERFORMANCE MANAGEMENT
Senior Leadership	3.2		
Supportive Culture	3.2	➡ 4.2	
Strategic Alignment	2.8		
Talent Assessment	3.1		
Performance Management	3.7		➡ 4.7
Learning and Development	3.2		
Human Resource Capabilities	3.3		
Talent Data Analytics	2.8		
Predicted Results Mean Score (Results – The Best Talent, Increased Diversity of Talent, Lower Cost, Improved Business Outcomes)	3.1	3.4	3.1

Figure 3.6

Now if we focus efforts on building a more Supportive Culture, we see that business outcomes improve by 10% (3.1 to 3.4)! The same can't be said for a one-point increase in Performance Management Processes and Systems. In fact, increasing Performance Management Processes and Systems one point has no effect on results.

While this type of talent research is quite useful for checking various scenarios within an organization, we need to keep in mind the interrelationship among the levers. As each lever does not exist in a vacuum, an increase in one area may likely have an impact in other areas. For instance, if we help an organization to increase senior leadership engagement and sponsorship, we will likely see an increase in supportive culture and strategic alignment, as these areas are highly connected to each other. The model is able to incorporate all of the interconnections simultaneously in a statistical manner that will measure not only individual contributions to results, but also combined impacts across the levers. We strongly believe that continued research in this area of talent optimization will yield significant benefits and insights.

Linking Stock Prices and External Measures of Success with the Talent Optimization Framework™

Another technique we utilized to test the TOF framework was to analyze the stock performance and accolades awarded to organizations representing the top quartile and bottom quartile in our research. We found strong relationships between TOF results and stock price (see Figure 3.7).

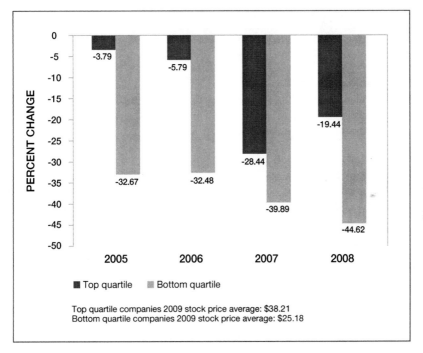

Figure 3.7

While top-quartile TOF organizations did not necessarily fare well in their stock movement in the period between 2005 and 2009, they significantly outperformed the organizations with bottom-quartile TOF scores. This provides additional evidence that a strong talent optimization approach is directly linked to business metrics.

In addition, we looked at published information regarding the best-in-class awards that companies in our study received. In particular, we looked at the number of times top-quartile and bottom-quartile TOF companies were mentioned on the following lists:

- Best Places to Work, *Fortune Magazine*
- Most Admired Companies, *Fortune Magazine*
- World's Most Sustainable Companies, *Forbes Magazine*

See what we found in Figure 3.8.

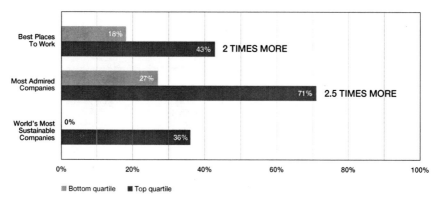

Figure 3.8

It is clear that organizations displaying strong TOF performance are far more likely to be recognized in publications as being elite and best-in-class. This provides additional confirmatory evidence of the relationship between talent optimization and performance.

Summary of Results

We set out to use data analytics to put our own talent framework to the test. What we found was encouraging:

- About 20% of organizations showed good strengths in their talent optimization efforts. There are role models out there to study and learn from.
- The TOF levers are highly correlated with measures of business outcomes.
- The assessment of an organization's culture is a must-do activity prior to launching a set of talent initiatives; a strong talent culture sets the foundation for improving talent practices.

- ▪ Strong talent assessment practices greatly enhance learning and development.
- ▪ Organizations with strong TOF results have better stock price movement and are much more likely to be viewed as "best," "most admired," or "most sustainable" places to work or companies as a whole.

In the following chapters, we guide you through each lever of the Talent Optimization Framework™. We explore the common talent practices that often damage an organizations ability to be talent rich, as well as the practices that support it. We provide real case studies from our deep experience. We suspect that you will be able to identify with many of these cases. Take the plunge and learn how you can optimize the talent of your organization.

CHAPTER 4

LEADERSHIP AND CULTURE

*The Glue that Holds the
Organization Together*

Optimizing Talent, pages 39–54

Leadership is tough. It is both an art and a science. It is engaging people's hearts and minds and working through them to deliver short- and long-term business results. The mind-numbing truth is that even with the thousands of books written about leadership, we leaders are still not walking the talk between what we say and what we do. We have seen many leaders who want to focus on only one aspect of their role while delegating or ignoring their other leadership responsibilities. Unfortunately, that's just not possible. As a leader, you cannot escape your unique role and position in the organization. If you want to be a leader, you have to have followers. Not just your own team, but others who you must influence to ensure that the strategic direction of the company is achieved. We used to talk about the criticality of managing and engaging teams of direct reports (Katzenbach and Smith, 1992). This is still critical, but today you must influence across business boundaries, functional lines, and geographies. It requires personal involvement to be a leader today and tomorrow. We know from our study that focusing on people is statistically correlated to improved performance, yet in pressured times leaders still don't do it. The question becomes, "Why?"

According to recent studies of organizations, bureaucratic models still linger. They have been adapted over time, but the roots of bureaucratic behavior still exist (particularly the negative aspects). Some would argue that these behaviors are the prevailing leadership style in most organizations. There are books written about "asshole bosses" whose behavior is controlling, demanding, inattentive, unresponsive, erratic, or characterized as "kissing up" and "kicking down" (Sutton, 2007). Sadly, we see far too many 360 feedback reports of various kinds that demonstrate the truth of this assertion. When such behavior is tolerated, it can be effective for the short-term, but it is toxic in the long-term. It is counterproductive and enervates followers (Morgan, 2006; Sutton, 2007).

In our interviews, human resource executives and company leaders still cite significant command-and-control behavior, despite their assertions that they are "actively trying" to move away from their command-and-control roots. This can be quite detrimental to the organization. To a certain extent, General Motors' failing was attributed to its reliance on this type of leadership style and the culture it created, which was slow, bureaucratic, and not innovative. And the CEO of Xerox acknowledges that the company's leadership style must change for it to succeed (Bryant, 2010).

According to Dr. Robert A. Cooke (1997), a leading expert on organizational culture and leaders' impact on followers, there are three types of cultures:

1. Passive/Defensive Culture: Encourages members to seek approval of others and be liked by others over producing high quality

goods and services. These cultures have members that conform to rules and do as they are told. They clear all decisions with superiors and try to avoid taking responsibility for actions or being blamed for mistakes.

2. Aggressive/Defensive Culture: Are autocratic in nature. These cultures encourage members to win at all costs and control others. Members avoid making mistakes and work long hours to keep on top of everything for little organizational payoff. These are highly critical cultures where members are constantly challenging one another in a negative way to outshine each other.

3. Constructive Culture (high performance): Encourages members to help each other achieve their personal and organizational goals. Members of this type of culture produce high quality products and services, are supportive of others, set challenging goals, and solve problems effectively. People are open with each other and there is a high degree of satisfaction with the work they do.

The Circumplex in Figure 4.1 is a model for these three types of culture.

Cooke (1997) also found that when asked what their ideal leadership impact should be, leaders' responses were the opposite of command-and-control approaches. The leaders he studied (over 5,000 globally) wanted an impact that was goal-focused, humanistic, and collaborative in nature. Leaders wanted to be more people-focused, but had difficulty getting away from defensive-aggressive and passive-aggressive styles of leadership. The following is an example of the culture disconnect of a company whose values indicate that they are high-performance and people-focused, but in reality has a culture that is much more command-and-control or passive-aggressive (see Figure 4.2).

Every CEO and leader reports regularly on the financials. Why aren't they doing the same relative to their people quality and people strategy? Sustainable organizations require and will continue to require the leadership of people, and we have discovered the critical behaviors that directly correlate to results. The key is not letting the tough times suck one back into old behaviors that are expedient for the short-term but destructive for the long-term.

In this chapter we will explore what leaders need to do to focus on the people equation and how an organization can develop and maintain this type of leadership. We will also demonstrate how a strong talent focus and culture of talent identification, development, and sharing are linked to positive business results. To a great degree, the leadership quandary around managing for results versus focusing on people can be answered simply with a resounding "Yes!" to both.

Members are expected to...

1 Be supportive and constructive in dealing with others

2 Be open and friendly and sensitive to the satisfaction of the work group

3 Agree with, gain the approval of, and be liked by others

4 Conform, follow the rules, and make a good impression

5 Do what they are told and clear all decisions with supervisors

6 Shift responsibilities to others and avoid being blamed for mistakes

7 Gain status and influence by being critical and constantly challenging one another

8 Take charge and "control" others and make decisions autocratically

9 Operate in a "win-lose" framework and work against peers to be noticed

10 Avoid making mistakes, work long hours, and keep "on top" of everything

11 Set challenging goals and solve problems effectively

12 Enjoy their work and produce high-quality products/services

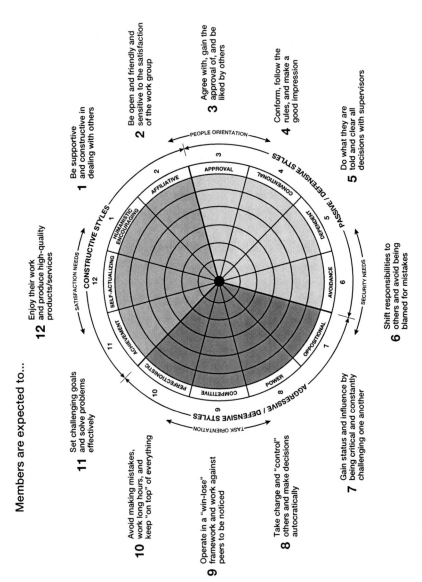

Figure 4.1 Quantifying Culture—The Circumplex. Copyright ©2010 by Human Synergistics International. All Rights Reserved.

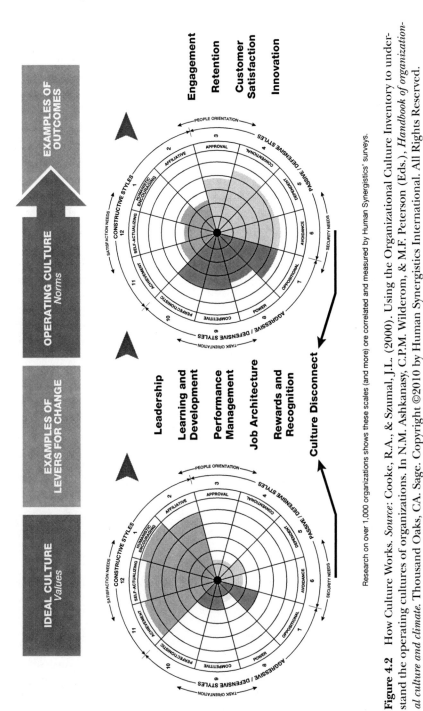

Figure 4.2 How Culture Works. *Source:* Cooke, R.A., & Szumal, J.L. (2000). Using the Organizational Culture Inventory to understand the operating cultures of organizations. In N.M. Ashkanasy, C.P.M. Wilderom, & M.F. Peterson (Eds.), *Handbook of organizational culture and climate.* Thousand Oaks, CA. Sage. Copyright ©2010 by Human Synergistics International. All Rights Reserved.

The Connection between Leadership and Culture

Our study of the relationship between leaders and organizational culture leads to the same conclusion as that of other well-respected scholars (Cooke, 1997; Trompenaars and Hampden-Turner, 1997), i.e., there is a strong correlation between leadership and culture. Our research showed that the elements of leadership engagement in talent acquisition and development were highly correlated with an organization's culture of talent development and talent sharing. Companies reporting that their leaders were actively engaged in talent optimization efforts displayed cultures that were also supportive of talent sustainability. In addition, these organizations reported much higher results for quality of talent, competitiveness, engagement, diversity, and bottom-line business results. Stephen I. Sadove, CEO of Saks Inc., summarizes it nicely, "A company's leaders set the tone for its culture, which in turn can lead to positive results... Culture drives innovation and whatever else you're trying to drive within a company.... And that then drives results" (Bryant, 2010).

As the following model shows, companies with constructive, high-performance, people-focused styles showed substantially higher engagement than companies that had defensive or passive leadership styles and cultures (see Figure 4.3).

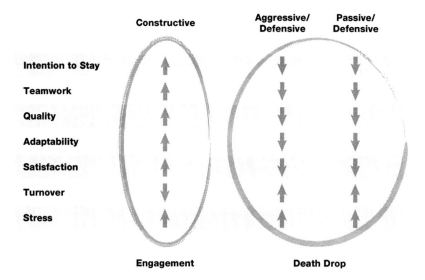

Figure 4.3   Why Constructive Culture Matters. Correlations from Szumal, J.L. (2001). *Reliability and Validity of the OEI.* Arlington Heights, IL: Human Synergistics/Center for Applied Research. Copyright ©2010 by Human Synergistics International. All Rights Reserved.

First, we know from our research that leadership and culture go hand in hand. What leaders do and how they behave create organizations that are talent rich, talent neutral, or talent poor. Why would any leader behave in a manner that leads the organization to be talent poor? The answer is that they lack the capacity *not* to behave in a manner that will lead the organization in that direction. In our hundreds of qualitative interviews with leaders in the executive suites of Fortune 500 companies, we heard the following themes consistently across the board:

1. I want to support my people to become great leaders. It is one of my top priorities.
2. I know that without an incredibly talented and engaged workforce, we will not be able to deliver for our shareholders.
3. As I climbed the ranks within my company, I could point to the leaders who took me under their wing and passed along their wisdom and advice to me. Without them, I would not be here today.
4. People are by far our most valued asset within the company.
5. I want my legacy to be the great leaders that I have helped develop and grow.

Not surprisingly, no leader interviewed made any mention or comment to indicate that talent development was not an important lever of success for his or her team or organization. So why do leadership behaviors so often contradict leadership words when it comes to talent and people development?

The answer is fairly simple: leaders tend to focus on what can be easily measured and what will have a measurable impact in the short term. Why wouldn't they? In today's ultra short-term world, we all live to a degree by the adage, "What have you done for me lately?" Those in leadership roles of any kind are expected to demonstrate positive, measurable results almost immediately. Being highly intelligent and well-educated, these business leaders quickly recognize that metrics around people and talent levers are few and far between and are often viewed as lagging indicators of results. This reinforces leadership behaviors that are short term and execution oriented. Behaviors are focused on taking the cost out of the equation, whether that means offshoring jobs, reducing headcount, increasing manager span of control, and of course reducing personal time and financial investments aimed at talent sustainability.

Let's examine some of these common contradictions between what leaders say and how they behave.

Leader Words

- It's the people who make the difference here
- People are our most important resource
- Giving frequent performance feedback and development opportunities to our people is critical
- How leaders behave is as important, if not more important, than the results they deliver
- We must make our people our competitive advantage
- We will be the best company at attracting top talent.

Leader Actions

- Participate in performance discussions once a year—and on occasion, replace the discussion with an email exchange
- Reward producers no matter how destructive their behaviors may be
- Hide their talented performers so that no one else in the organization may find them
- Invest little if any time in coaching or developing team members
- Overload employees with work activities so that there is no time for development experiences
- Treat talent like it is an expendable commodity—a warm body that can be easily replaced by another warm body.

Without leadership behaviors and actions supporting talent sustainability initiatives, the likelihood of success is drastically reduced. Great leaders are those who focus on the talent equation of their teams and organizations. If you want to be sure that you have the leadership you need to sustain your talent over time, you must look at the culture that you have created, assess the leadership characteristics that have created it, and focus on those that must be either changed or maintained to support or improve that culture.

Some senior leaders have asked us, "Why does everything start with the leaders?" Our simple answer is, "Because it does!" Let's explore this case study of a large company. The CEO operated with a list of 20 projects that she was tracking. These were tactical projects and probably linked to the overall strategy of the company, but if they were, few knew it. This CEO wanted to know why everything had to start with her: *because it does.* Narrowing the focus to the most important elements of what is needed to drive change and sustain the enterprise over the long haul *IS* the leader's job. This leader needs to be a representative of the issues that matter to the company's success, not managing the tactical parts of the company. Others are paid to do those things and for a leader to do so could be considered "micromanagement."

It's the leader's job to signal through his or her actions what is important and how it connects with the company strategy. The leader's job is complex and requires strong people involvement. This is just one reason why leaders are paid the "big bucks." Project managers manage multiple projects and the tactics connected with them, and for far less money than leaders.

The second aspect of good leaders is leading the human side of the organization. No enterprise leader would command a company without a strong financial plan, clear strategy, or creative marketing plan. Why would they not have an equally strong people strategy with appropriate vision, analytics, accountabilities, and links to the bottom line?

This is not a book about leadership theory, so we will not go into the details here other than to highlight some of the relevant facts. It is clear, though, that a sustainable enterprise needs four types of plans that are linked and aligned:

1. Financial Plan: outlining the details of the margins, segments, revenue projections, etc.
2. Strategic Plan: defining go-to-market approaches, competitive activity, future market opportunities, new products, and value propositions.
3. Marketing Plan: covering market segments of customers, buying patterns, trends, future needs.
4. Talent Plan: outlining skills for current and future business requirements, analytics for performance, and impact and return on investment (ROI) of people plans.

Leaders must know their talent, they must understand the culture they are creating, and they must have a leadership style that leverages other people.

Why Is Culture So Important to Talent Optimization?

Culture is the invisible glue that sets the tone for the organization, highlights how decisions are made, and underscores what is valued. There is a widely circulated story about monkeys, presumably based on research done in the 1970s, that correlates with corporate behavior and culture.

A team of monkeys was put into a room and each morning a fresh batch of bananas was hung in front of them. Each time a monkey went to get a banana, it would get squirted with water by a researcher. This went on for a while until no monkeys went after a banana even though new fresh bananas were presented each day. The bananas would rot on the plate. None of the monkeys would try to take one. At intervals, the researchers would take out one monkey and put in a new one that had never been squirted when reaching for a banana. When the new monkey tried to take one of the nice lush bananas, it was squirted. This happened for a day or two, but very quickly the new monkey would learn that going after the bananas was not a rewarding move. Eventually all of the monkeys were changed out of the group, but the behavior of not taking the risk to get a banana prevailed. No monkeys, regardless of their time in the group, dared taking a banana. The lesson here is that the culture was transmitted monkey-to-monkey and they were somehow telling each other, "Don't go after the bananas you'll get squirted." Soon, the culture became entrenched.

While leaders and their followers aren't monkeys, the analogies are too similar to ignore. If leaders continue to "squirt" (punish) subordinates when they come up with ideas or ask for feedback or coaching, the subordinates will eventually stop asking and do exactly what they are told without question. Think about your own organizations: How much risk are you encouraged to take, and how often does someone whisper in your ear, "If you want to be successful around here, don't rock the boat!" Leaders are the role models of a culture's values and if the value is not to take risks, followers eventually get the message and do as they are told—without being "told" in so many words. With this little story, we hope to have highlighted for you the important fact that leaders create the culture and cultures can inhibit or enable organizational growth.

As previously discussed, we are seeing a lot of instances of the defensive aggressive (characterized as command-and-control) styles of cultures and leader behavior. The following case study describes what this type of culture feels like and what leaders do to create it.

A company's leadership team has a pattern of bringing in subordinates to make presentations on the status of their business or function. When the person or team presents, the leadership team members are highly critical, find fault, and are abusive in language and rude in behavior. They often send the presenters back for more data and detail, causing people to work long hours for very limited return. The followers have a great sense of fear of attending these meetings and know their careers can be on the line if they make even a slight misstep. They do whatever they can to make sure that they are not seen as wrong or making a mistake. Often they burn out from the long and tedious work hours. The message they get from their leaders is clear: 1)If you wish to survive, don't help others, help yourself; 2) Make sure you never take blame; and 3) Always try to outperform your peers. The organization's culture and its leaders are focused solely on the tasks of the organization at the expense of the people equation.

More often than not, organizations of this type have slogans on their walls calling for more innovation, teamwork, and customer focus to solve customer issues. But none of these are going to happen. People are too afraid to step outside expected behaviors and norms. The saddest part isn't that there is no growth, no innovation, and no teamwork at this type of organization; it's that the leaders have no idea that they are having this stifling, debilitating impact on their followers. Our research has made the case for leadership that drives results through effective people skills.

What Is It that Leaders Do that Creates a High-Performance, Talent-Focused Culture that Is Correlated with Results?

First and foremost, leaders who create a high-performance culture that is correlated with results are visibly and actively engaged in talent initiatives. They have clear talent goals that cascade throughout the organization. Leaders actively support these goals, not merely pay them lip service. Two examples of such leadership come to mind.

The first organization, Unilever, has a clear culture-of-talent focus. Leaders see it as their responsibility to pay attention to and develop their talent. They deliberately move talent around. It is part of their DNA and has been for a long time. The second such company is General Electric. There, leaders are chief talent officers and moving around to different positions in the company to gain experience is just one way that leaders are developed (Welch and Byrne, 2003).

Apart from being visibly and actively engaged in talent initiatives, leaders who create high-performing cultures have the following consistent habits, which they NEVER deviate from, even in times of crisis:

- **Effectively assess, develop, and coach talent**. Leaders make accurate assessments of talent against their values and expected leader behaviors. They provide clear, specific statements about an individual's strengths and needs. They never revert to vague statements like "good guy," "delivers on numbers," or "gets along well with others." Rather, they are articulate about an individual's abilities and can describe them in ways that are clear and observable. Examples might be, "Joe is excellent at delegating to his team. He provides clear criteria about what is expected, time frames to accomplish expectations, and gives regular coaching to the team so that they stay on track." Leaders with good assessment skills are better equipped to give positive coaching that helps people improve by knowing exactly what they have to do to improve. Coaching is a cornerstone of development. We found from our survey that this factor alone had a very strong and positive relationship with business results.

▪ **Move talent based upon business need and personal aspirations**. This factor is critical to knowing your talent. Often we find companies that move talent, but in the absence of career aspirations. There is a specific case that comes to mind in which a company had a business need and convinced an employee to take the position. The employee did not want the position, but took the job to be a good corporate citizen. He delivered on expectations. The job then had new requirements, which the employee did not have. The company no longer had a need for the individual in the role and he was out of his area of expertise and could not find another role. Eventually, he was let go at great cost to the company (from a monetary perspective) and to him (from a reputation perspective). This situation could clearly have been avoided if there was alignment between company needs and employee aspirations or a plan in place for how to deal with the employee's career after the requested assignment was over. Unfortunately, this scenario happens all too often.

▪ **Assume accountability for having and delivering on talent plans**. This is the area where we still hear that so much time is spent in structured talent reviews or analysis and very little happens as a result. It is akin to the strategic plan dilemma: create the plan, put it in a drawer, and never let it see the light of day again. In marked contrast, companies like McDonalds, IBM, Cisco, and Unilever make their talent plans live and actively use the plans to make talent decisions. These organizations revisit these plans frequently in talent discussions. Leaders have clear succession plans and are accountable for developing their successor.

▪ **Act as communication champions for talent initiatives.** These individuals serve as a champion for talent on their teams and ensure they get the experiences they need to advance in their careers. They do not delegate to HR the responsibility of recruiting talent, but personally seek out talent and help to develop it. The CEO of a large credit card company is a prime example. Everywhere she goes she is actively scouting talent and personally getting to know people, whether or not she currently has a role for them in her organization. She is someone people go to when they have a role to fill for talent ideas. This CEO also does another important thing: she champions her team. She thinks ahead about what their next move should be and she reaches out to hiring managers so they get to know her team. Then when the time is right, her team members can easily find their next best role. She also has a reputation for developing great talent. She is truly people focused and delivers results.

- **Are personally engaged in leadership development initiatives**. These leaders never stand in the way of someone gaining a development experience. They don't make it hard for team members to go to required or appropriate training. They are not constantly calling them out of class. These leaders make it clear that development is important. They actively model development themselves. A case in point: a very senior leader who had difficulty making presentations to large audiences actively sought out coaching. He told everyone what he was doing to improve and sought feedback about how his presentations had benefitted. This individual became an excellent keynote presenter. He worked hard to perfect a skill in an area in which he was uncomfortable, signaling to his organization that personal development was important even when it was tough.

How Do Leaders Develop a Supportive Culture for Talent?

To build a supportive culture, leaders must develop a transparent organization where values are clear and the behaviors that support those values are modeled and understood at all levels. No one is exempt from living out the values, no matter who they are. In one company, a top producer once was heard to say, "I don't have to collaborate with others [even though this was a strong company value], because I bring in top revenue myself. No one can make me change and I am not going to change." This signaled to everyone else that it was okay to ignore the organization's values, that they were merely platitudes that applied to some and not others. In another company, the CEO made a visible example of what happens if a leader ignores the values. In this particular case, the CEO fired the leader, and it was made very clear why the leader was let go. Every time someone is hired or promoted who does not actively live the organization's values, the message being given is that values are not important.

Here are some other actions that leaders use to develop a supportive culture for talent:

- Value diversity of thought, background, style, and idea. They are not constrained by their own view of the world and they actively seek out other perspectives. Leaders we know who embrace this trait have incredibly diverse teams. They don't have to be educated about the "business case" for diversity; they recognize its value and actively pursue it.
- Have a high degree of candor that is felt across the organization. Employees know where they stand and how they are evaluated. They understand what they need to do to improve. If they are failing, they know that, too. Let's contrast two organizations. The first organization has an open and transparent culture. If an employee is not making it in a position and has generally been a good employee in previous positions, the leader will discuss the challenges with the employee openly. A clear agreement is made about what the next steps will be, including leaving the company if appropriate. Honest efforts are made to help the employee into an appropriate position either within or outside the company. There are no surprises. The second organization tells employees that they are valued and then secretly searches for a replacement. Leaders tell the employee that he or she is being replaced or moved days before the change is to occur. Imagine how much trust exists in the culture of the second company—it's not much!
- Encourage movement across the organization. Leaders do not hoard talent for their own needs. They actively share talent so that both the people and the company can grow. The value of developing people for the greater good of the organization is strong.
- Are willing to test out new ideas. They value testing new ways of doing things and encourage risk taking. Employees are not blamed or punished if they try something new and it does not work out perfectly.
- Help the organization become branded as a place that develops leaders.

How Do You Achieve and Sustain Leadership Engagement and a Supportive Culture?

First and foremost, you are clear about your values and make sure that everyone understands them. Address any potential blind spots relative to how you live these values and take bold action to close the gaps. Do not allow anyone a "pass" on what is important, no matter how much revenue they bring in. Pay attention to your culture. Keep a pulse on your employee attitudes. If engagement starts to slip, find out why and fix it. Make no excuses. Finally, ask yourself the following questions and rate yourself on a 1–10 scale (with 1 being the lowest and 10 being highest):

- Do others know your values and what you stand for?
- Do you operate consistently with your values? How do you know?
- Do you coach your employees to be the best they can be?
- Are you visible when it comes to developing talent?
- Do you participate in development programs?
- Do you seek out talent and help promote careers?
- Do you "walk the talk" and seek feedback about how you are doing?
- Do you work on your own self-development?
- Do you give honest feedback so that people who work with and for you know where they stand?
- Do you actively communicate your company leadership brand in the marketplace?

If you got gold medal scores on the above questions, congratulations! You're an Olympian! If not, you have some work to do. Go get the facts, find the gaps, define a strategy, and take action. Use valid instruments to determine where you are; communicate the results so that everyone knows the issues; share the strategy. And, most importantly, communicate, communicate, communicate regularly on progress. If you think you have communicated enough, communicate more. You can never communicate enough about what is important. Tell stories to highlight what you value and give specific examples so others know what is expected of them. Measure consistently and regularly so you can see progress and share that progress openly. If there have been setbacks, be honest about them and what you plan to do about them. This is not easy, but it is the call of leadership and the mark of a great leader. As Malcolm Gladwell (2008) put it, "What makes people great at what they do is practice." Practice today, practice tomorrow, and practice in the future and you will become a gold medal Olympian at leadership.

References

Bryant, A. (2010, February 20). Xerox's new chief tries to redefine its culture. *The New York Times*, p. BU1. Retrieved September 10, 2010, from http://www.nytimes.com/2010/02/21/business/21xerox.html?_r=1&scp=2&sq=xerox&st=nyt

Cooke, R. A. (1997). *Leadership/Impact feedback report.* Plymouth, MI: Human Synergistics International.

Gladwell, M. (2008). *Outliers: The story of success.* New York: Little, Brown and Company.

Katzenbach, J. R., & Smith, D. K. (1992). *The wisdom of teams: Creating the high-performance organization.* Boston: Harvard Business Press.

Morgan, G. (2006). *Images of organization.* Thousand Oaks, CA: Sage Publications.

Sutton, R. (2007). *The no asshole rule.* New York: Business Plus.

Trompenaars, F., & Hampden-Turner, C. (1997). *Riding the waves of culture: Understanding diversity in global business* (2nd ed.). New York: McGraw-Hill.

Welch, J., & Byrne, J. A. (2003). *Jack: Straight from the gut.* New York: Business Plus.

CHAPTER 5

STRATEGIC ALIGNMENT
The Underpinnings of the Organization

Optimizing Talent, pages 55–63
Copyright © 2011 by Information Age Publishing
All rights of reproduction in any form reserved.

With so many different business strategies and numerous books about strategy already published, we are not going to recommend how to develop your strategy. Rather, in this chapter, we are going to discuss the link between strategy, people, and performance.

Strategy should be the roadmap for providing direction to the company. It should ensure that everyone is headed in the same direction and/ or generally staying within the company "guardrails" for what it is trying to achieve. One thing is clear: every organization needs a sense of purpose around which to define its strategy, i.e, what the organization is about, what it provides to customers, what it wants to be known for, what markets it plays in, what markets it needs to expand into, what its core competencies are, what values it will live by, and how it will measure performance.

Such strategies take many forms and have a range of options. From having a strong "growth playbook" to having a mission statement with supporting goals or principles, or a vision that everyone knows, whatever strategy or approach is chosen, it must be one that guides the company to its "true north."

Without strategy and purpose, a company can wander from initiative to initiative, never capturing its true value. Without a clear statement of purpose, organizations lose their ability to learn what's working and what isn't. Once a company loses its thirst for learning, it becomes stagnant.

Purpose has to have an emotional hook for the members of an organization in order for them to follow through. People need answers to questions that affect them personally, such as, "What are we all about? Why am I here at this organization? What's in it for me and my values?" This last question is particularly important as a new generation of employees enters the workforce. Employees of the younger generation want to know what the organization stands for, what it values, and ultimately what is expected of them and the leaders to whom they report (Mourkogiannis and Fisher, 2006).

Once you are clear on the organization's purpose, mission, vision, and goals, however you articulate them in your organization, you must understand the people implications. We have said it before and we'll say it again—strategy is essential, but without understanding the people component, a strategy is merely a document. Without an understanding of your ability to execute on the strategy from a people perspective and how you will measure performance against it, it won't go anywhere.

The People-Strategy-Performance Link: Framework

Some would say you need to understand your people capability first, then understand what you can do relative to strategy. As Collins (2009) says, get the best people and then get your strategy. Our experience would argue that first you must understand where you need to head as a company and then you need to examine whether you have the right capability to execute the strategy. Whichever way you choose to approach the strategy question, you must link the people to your ability to execute the strategy.

So, where do you start? We believe that strategic alignment is comprised of three things:

1. Clear purpose
2. Values
3. People who can execute the purpose and embody the values

Most people say that strategy—however it is defined—should be the underpinning of the company, that the leaders need to be able to deliver on it, and that people and strategy should be linked. However, we have found relatively few leaders who know how to link the two successfully.

Once you have established the purpose and values that are important to the organization, the next step is to set a game plan for delivering on them. Most companies are adept at doing some form of this, although very few take the next step of aligning leader capabilities to the strategy to see if they have the right talent for the job today and for the future. Most companies examine their leadership talent by looking at individual performance—using a performance rating and evaluation of potential (*potential* most often being defined as some form of skills, ability to show the values, or a sense of intelligence that the company believes shows the capacity to take on larger more complex roles). The basis for decisions about potential is usually pretty general and therefore flawed, offering limited insight for action. It often does nothing to help people understand what they need to do differently to advance unless they are deemed top talent. Performance ratings can be flawed in this way as well, particularly if they don't reflect alignment with the future strategy of the company. This is easier said than done and we will discuss it in further detail when we get to the chapter on performance management.

For now, let's look at a mini case example. A major company tries to link its strategy, people, and performance in rounds of discussions leaders have about their talent. In this case, the company does not have an overarching set of goals or a strategy to review the performance aspect and leaders are not clear on the values that they profess to embrace. Thus, the review discussions are done in a siloed fashion and based upon the individual business unit's goals and not linked to the overall direction of the company. If a business unit has clear goals and some view of who is good and who is not, they pass the test and move forward with their plans. But what is this doing for the overall good of the company? Not surprisingly, if the strategy is siloed, the talent will also be siloed. This is one of the deadly sins of talent management and business strategy. It happens unwittingly, stemming from a flawed view of how organizations work.

Another often-heard point about "talent management" (Ugh! There's that *management* word again) is that it "starts with the business strategy." Nearly every talent book written repeats this same point. However, we have yet to see anyone who explains how you do this in a quantifiable way. If your talent needs to be aligned to your strategic demands, then you need to know how to get that alignment. Period.

Here is an example of how this can be done. Senior leaders of a well-known company took their business strategy and broke it down into critical components that were actionable. They needed one face to show to the customer and a seamless process to do this that went across the organization. They also wanted to be known for creative solutions and thinking outside the box when it came to customer needs. Sound familiar?

What was the solution? How did they dissect these strategic elements so that they ultimately reflected the behaviors required to run the business? The company in the example held a facilitated retreat with their most senior leaders, who spent a day defining what was required of them if they were to be more customer-focused and creative in how they approached their work. This had broader implications for how these leaders worked with their staff and developed their people.

Out of this one-day session, during which the strategy was dissected for leadership requirements that reflected the future needs of the company, a formal leadership framework emerged. This framework was then broken down into specific skills that would visibly show the elements of the framework. Now the organizational development people could do their work! Once the leaders embraced the requirements needed for the future, this framework and the necessary skills could be tested, put into a behaviorally anchored scale, and documented to determine the skills capability of the organization and ultimately the performance requirements.

We use the following model to help companies assess market realities through their organizational lens. We then determine the specific skills that leaders will need if they are to function well in the market today and in the future[1] (see Figure 5.1).

---

1. We engage the leaders in a dialogue around this model to help them determine trends and leadership implications. We use a very effective leader-of-the-future exercise developed by Linda Sharkey for GE. It is based upon the early thoughts of Jim Kouzes and Barry Posner (1995). The exercise is included in the chapter 5 appendix.

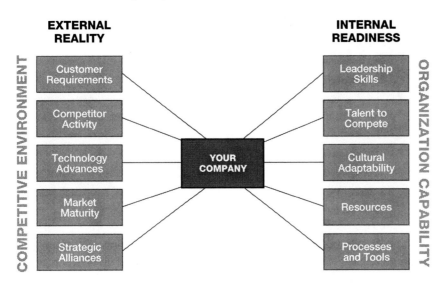

Figure 5.1 Organization Capability Map.

The beauty of this approach is that the framework and skills required reflected the unique characteristics of the company and its values, all of which was articulated in language that the senior leaders embraced. Every leader in the room could state why these skills were important to the strategy and the business. Unbeknownst to them, they left the retreat with their "elevator speech." Using this approach provided real consensus in the organization about what was important.

This is a critical step that cannot be circumvented. Every decision made and action taken from this point, relative to talent, hinges on what the leaders decide are the most important attributes that organizational talent must possess to be successful today and tomorrow.

Now let's examine another very successful company that undertook a similar exercise. However, leadership delegated this activity to consultants and to the human resource development staff. The staff and consultants looked at various competency models and existing assessment tools. They researched and analyzed the strategy for clues about skills requirements. They came back with the recommendation for what the framework should be.

What's wrong with the picture portrayed by this company? At least three things:

1. Top leaders are not personally engaged in defining what THEY think is important—they delegate it to others. As demonstrated

in the previous chapter, companies whose leaders are personally engaged in talent activities had a very strong correlation with high performance. Delegating this engagement to human resources loses much of the power and punch.

2. Top leaders have not internalized the skills they believe are necessary and, more likely than not, will neither remember them nor reinforce them. They have gone through the motions but have no visceral commitment.

3. The company will likely take these identified skills and build assessments, training, and more around them, and they may not even be relevant to top leaders down the road!

This is very costly on a number of fronts, for not only will talent processes be flawed, but money will be spent on developing skills that may not really be important to leadership, which will seriously affect the bottom line of the organization in the future.

Let's look at a vivid example of the impact of not having leaders aligned and actively engaged in the development of leadership requirements and skills. A company was having an all-employee meeting and the CEO leading the meeting reiterated at least five times how she did not believe in vision statements and thought they were a waste of time. Prominent in the company's leadership model was the ability to set a clear and compelling vision. This was an obvious disconnect. Leaders were being assessed on their ability to create a vision and visioning exercises were a cornerstone of leadership development efforts, but top leadership was not supportive of this. This confusing message led to less and less attention being paid to the ability to create a vision—supposedly a key component of the company's leadership model.

In another case, a CEO did not believe in coaching. He had a bad experience with one of his subordinates who had had a coach. He was a proponent of the theory that leaders are born, not developed. However, coaching was a central part of the company's leadership model! Again, a very disconnected message was sent out, which confused employees and thus stunted the progress of the organization. Though these CEOs were unaware of the disconnect they were creating, the negative effect on the talent in their organizations was undeniable. Getting the framework and competencies right is essential for a robust talent system to work.

The People-Strategy-Performance Link: Performance versus Potential

Once you have the framework in place and the linkages can be mapped directly to the company strategy and values, you are ready to begin work on phase two of developing your people-strategy-performance link.

Questions to ask as you begin this second phase are:

- What do these competencies look like when they are at their best and what do they look like when they are not fully formed? Garnering the answers to these questions is often the work of human resources professionals and consultants and there are many "best practices" here.
- What are the measures and language that will be used to assess the key competencies?

Once this framework is boiled down to its various shades of poor to excellent, it becomes very clear what excellent performance looks like and what poor performance looks like, as well as all shades in-between. This gives leaders anchors against which to do an objective and thorough assessment of their staff. Additionally, talent knows exactly what they need to do to improve in very specific ways. It takes the guesswork out of performance discussions and feedback sessions.

Now, poised to have an informed discussion about performance versus potential, you can more readily determine who your "stars" are, who needs development, and who may not succeed in the company over the long term. A caution: while strategies evolve over time and these models should be revised and revisited on a regular basis to ensure they are current and forward-focused, constant transformation and shifting of strategic priorities are a sure sign of the death spiral. As Jim Collins (2009) said so well: Companies that are in constant search of the silver bullet, "churning through management teams.... lurching from strategy to strategy and program to program looking for fundamental transformation," have failed.

Smart companies that endure view strategy, talent, and performance as interlinked. In a systematic way, they constantly assess where their strategic "sweet spot" is. They do the same relative to their talent. To further make this point, we are reminded of a company in Denmark that was extremely systematic in its approach to staying ahead of the competition. They weren't arrogant about their position in the market. They wanted to "catch the wave." In other words, when one wave reached its peak, they wanted to start

Figure 5.2 Riding the wave to stay great. *Source*: Adapted from Jim Collins, *How the Mighty Fall.*

riding the next wave to its peak, not get caught in the vortex of the first wave as it crashed (see Figure 5.2).

The same principle applies to people. You've realized by now that your talent system is an interlinked system. What happens in one area feeds or affects another. Leaders have to be constantly looking at all parts of the TOF to ensure that all elements are in sync with the strategy, making adjustments as necessary in order to keep the people systems fresh and capable of riding the wave to the next pinnacle. As Marshall Goldsmith (2007b) puts it, "What got you here won't get you there," i.e., people must continue to change and adjust throughout their careers in order to continue to ride the wave of success.

At this point, think about your checklist for the success of your talent process. Reflect on the following questions:

- Does your talent process have behaviors linked to your business strategy and values?
- Have your key leaders been actively engaged in the process?
- Do you own the leadership framework?
- Do you believe that it embodies the characteristics required for leaders of the future?
- Have you boiled down the characteristics to observable, quantifiable behaviors?

- Do you know what "excellent" looks like and can you clearly articulate that?
- Do you have a clear vision and purpose for your talent strategy that can be easily articulated and understood by the organization as a whole?

If you answered "yes" to the questions above, you are ready to move on to the next phase of the model—assessments.

References

Collins, J. (2009). *How the mighty fall: And why some companies never give in.* Author.

Goldsmith, M. (2007b). *What got you here won't get you there: How successful people become even more successful!* New York: Hyperion.

Mourkogiannis, N., & Fisher, P. (2006). *Purpose: The starting point of great companies.* New York: Palgrave Macmillan.

APPENDIX 5:
SMALL GROUP DISCUSSION:
DEFINING THE LEADER OF THE FUTURE

Outcomes:
* Identify business challenges, industry trends, and customer needs.
* Identify the most critical characteristics and actions to be possessed by leaders of the future.
* Arrive at a group consensus on the most critical actions for leaders of the future.

Instructions:
* Individually review the responses you received from your manager, your peers, and your external customers regarding the organizational challenge pre-work questions. Complete the "Leader of the Future" grid that follows.
* Think about the following questions as you complete the last row of the grid.

    * Based on how the organization will respond, what will be required of its leaders two or three years from now?
    * What behaviors will be most critical for leaders to demonstrate in order to meet the challenges of the next two or three years?

* Get together in small groups to discuss what you believe are the key challenges, trends, customer needs, as well as how the organization needs to respond to them. Discuss what leaders need to do to meet these challenges and identify the core behaviors that, as a group, you feel all leaders will need to exhibit. Work to develop a consensus on the leadership actions required; this becomes your "Leader of the Future" model.

* Choose one person to report out what your group defines as the "key leadership actions" required for the future.

TOOL: LEADER OF THE FUTURE GRID

		DATA FROM PRE-WORK
1	Customer needs and expectations	
2	Industry trends over the next 2 to 3 years	
3	Business challenges over the next 2 to 3 years	
4	How the organization needs to respond	
5	Personal Leadership Challenges	
	What will leaders need to do to meet these challenges?	

CHAPTER 6

TALENT ASSESSMENT

The People-Strategy-Performance Link

Optimizing Talent, pages 65–84

Assessments mean different things to different people, and there are many different types of assessments used within companies. There is the talent review assessment, which we discussed in the business strategy chapter. Usually done yearly, the performance and potential of talent are plotted on a grid to determine who is top talent and who may need to be moved. These grids come in many forms. One of the most popular is the 9-box model used by General Electric. Some organizations use a 4-box model; others use a plot chart to determine relative rankings of talent, and others use pure top-to-bottom rankings. All of these methods include an axis for performance, which is typically the performance rating of an employee and some view of his or her potential. These are methods commonly used to ferret out the best from the worst and to determine who are the "high potentials" in the organization. With these methods, companies recognize the "hi-pos," the muddle in the middle, and the ones who are underperforming—but that's often as far as it goes.

Another type of assessment is succession planning. In succession planning, critical jobs are identified and an assessment is made relative to who is ready for that role now, should the position open, and if you have talent in the pipeline.

The focus of this chapter will be on individual assessments, which provide an employee with a full view of his or her strengths and challenges. These types of assessments are typically done in leadership programs and executive coaching, i.e., for the top tier of the company. Rarely are they done systematically and for all leadership positions across an organization.

We contend that it is very difficult to conduct a thorough talent review discussion, to complete a talent grid effectively, or to do an effective succession plan without conducting an in-depth individual assessment of a leader. Without this, however, the assessment is just a gut view of an individual's talent. This is not reliable, as criteria for making decisions about who has longer-term potential can vary dramatically depending on who is doing the assessing and what criteria they are using. This point alone often renders the results of the talent reviews discussed above flawed. The following case study makes our point. This sobering story underscores what happens when assessments are not done systematically and when leaders don't have the best assessment skills.

A major Fortune 100 company had gone through its yearly talent review cycle and determined who the star performers were that they wanted to retain. They then sent these stars to several prestigious leadership development programs to further enhance their skills. At the training program, formal assessments were used as part of the development process. Everyone in the organization knew that leaders selected to attend these programs were considered top talent in the company.

After reviewing the assessments from the training program, it became clear that about 10% of the populations deemed "high performers" were in fact "toxic" leaders. They did not embody the values of the company. In fact, they were quite the opposite! The traditional yearly cycles of talent reviews and succession plans had a very large margin of error. Figure 6.1 shows that there is a clear margin of error of 10%.[1] While some might say that 10% is not too bad, think about this fact. Each one of these leaders had 10 direct reports and influenced about 500 to 1,000 people in their business or functional unit. Employees who reported to these leaders heard the words of the CEO about what was expected of their leaders, but saw very different behavior on a day-to-day basis. This is not the message any company wants to send. To paraphrase a respected CEO, whom you hire and promote speaks volumes about what you value and think is important in leaders: choose your talent carefully because it signals a lot about you as a leader. The employees reporting to the poor leaders had reason to be cynical and disgruntled as they did not see the leadership that they expected. The result of the cynicism and dissatisfaction was, naturally, lower performance, disengagement, and turnover. We think this case makes our point. These talent processes are only as effective as the data and criteria used to determine quality and capability of the talent.

What follows is a discussion of individual assessments, how to do them well, and how to use them effectively to increase the quality of your talent pool and review process, and performance and coaching discussions. We believe that good assessment is about good individual assessment—it will change how you do talent reviews and succession planning forever.

Why Do Individual Assessments?

We've made a strong case for the power of assessment already in this book. Assessments validate beliefs about talent and provide an objective basis upon which to make decisions about the leadership capability of an individual manager. Basically, an assessment puts science into your talent processes and enables you to determine patterns in leadership styles much like you would with customers. Any way you look at it, without assessments, mistakes

---

1. Figure 6.1 is based on the Leadership/Impact™, a valid and reliable instrument developed by Dr. Robert A Cooke (1997) that measures leadership behavior and cultural impact on employees. For more about the Circumplex, see chapter 4.)

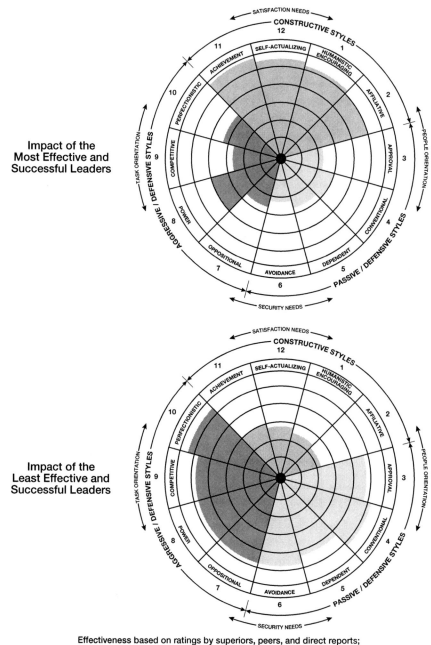

Impact of the
Most Effective and
Successful Leaders

Impact of the
Least Effective and
Successful Leaders

Effectiveness based on ratings by superiors, peers, and direct reports;
success based on performance-based salary increases over time.

Figure 6.1 Actual Impact Varies. Top 10% vs. bottom 10% within a major corporation. Copyright ©2010 by Human Synergistics International. All Rights Reserved.

are made and you will likely lose a great talent either because they slip in performance in the stretch role or they go elsewhere because they want to be great at what they love doing.

Assessments give you insight into the particular and personal sweet spots of your talent. They help ensure that you have the right person in the right role at the right time. Individual assessments are the critical building blocks for your talent strategy. In a nutshell, assessments will provide some if not all of the following:

- Best-in-class profiles for recruiting and hiring from the outside
- The basis for promoting from within
- A picture of the skills the company values in its leaders
- Consistent and aggregate picture of skills in the organization and what skills are missing that may be essential for success
- Objective fodder for talent discussions
- A basis for performance reviews
- The foundation for development and coaching
- Aligned career planning and career decision making
- Underpinnings for succession planning
- Measurement of progress in building required skills and the opportunity to conduct talent analytics—specifically, to quantify the skills most correlated with business results
- Onboarding plans for new hires and promoted employees
- Accurate information about whether to "buy or build" a particular skill set

In addition, assessments done well are the jumping-off point for most people processes.

A cautionary note about using 360 surveys: while they were the tool of the 20th century, they are insufficient for the 21st. We are not saying that quantifiable 360s are bad, but they need to be augmented with behavioral-based interviews and scenarios that will decipher exactly what the person does well, what they need to improve, and how they will react in certain circumstances. All assessments, to some degree, reflect the perception of others about the assessee. However, without a skilled assessor able to probe and ask more specific questions to clarify and verify numeric answers, the 360 scores can be misleading or inflated. Until an organization can clearly assess why one leader is a high potential and another is not, its talent system will be flawed and ineffective and not yield the talent gains desired.

Using Assessment for Recruitment and Promotions

Assessing and attempting to measure talent is not simple. With so much about talent hidden beneath the surface, it is often a mystery how to identify and develop it. It can seem impossible to look at the make-up of a job candidate and discern whether the candidate will have what it takes to succeed within the job, the team, and the company culture. Studies indicate that new hires into leadership roles come in with great promise, but all too often leave or are asked to leave within the first18 months of the new assignment (Wheeler, 2010). Headhunters charge astronomical fees based on promises of finding and securing an organization's talent. However, the results from these promises are often disappointing.

You may be asking yourself, "How is this possible?" We frame the question a bit differently, "Why doesn't it happen even more often?" The truth is that the manner in which most of us approach hiring new talent into our teams and organizations is similar to throwing darts in the dark, or choosing spouses based on a round or two of speed dating.

Here's how it typically happens in organizations: a manager finds herself with an opening on the team and immediately feels the pressure to get the job filled. With great enthusiasm, the best of intentions, and a dose of fear, our manager gets after the task of hiring a highly talented person for the job, that right talent that will make life easier for everyone on the team. Job ads are created, candidates are phone screened, and interviews are set up. Our manager is excited to see progress—a few special candidates float to the top like cream. One final round of interviews after which a winner will be declared. Perhaps it's a luncheon interview to get a feel for rapport or a group interview to see which candidate can stand up to the pressure of the team. Yes, she decides, this is the way to go.

Our manager gathers three team members to participate in the final interview. After introductions, the questions and answers bounce back and forth like a tennis ball at Wimbledon.

- Finalist one—good with the serve, strong handshake, excellent first impression on the team, weaker on the return game, stumbles on some of the tougher questions.
- Finalist two—mediocre serve, a little meek during introductions, but what a return! Handles questions with ease; up for a baseline rally.
- Finalist three—the whole package: personality, funny anecdotes, similar background as the team. This person handles the team's best shots with confidence and clarity. A clear winner is found.

The job is offered and accepted. Our manager is pleased and relieved to have filled the role with such a "good guy."

Three months into the job, the first warning signs are evident. Our new hire isn't ramping up very quickly. He always seems to say the right things. He is pleasant and attentive to instructions, but he hasn't delivered anything yet. Our manager preaches patience, "Remember, at one time or another, we were all rookies around here."

Month six: there is no improvement. This person makes lots of commitments but is not much on the delivering side. There is lots of eloquent talk, but limited action. "It is time for a midyear review," thinks our manager. "I'll use this session as a pep talk and get the new guy turned around."

Month twelve: there is still no improvement. Our manager is frustrated. She sits in her office pondering the inevitable, "I need to launch this loser. Who recommended this guy anyway?" Alas, the cycle continues. It is time to start the search process once again.

Classic Talent Assessment Errors

We all make mistakes assessing people. Whether it is the general contractor we hired to do some home updates who whiled away the days watching football in our basement, or the babysitter who spent her evenings with our children unattended as she mastered her Facebook skills on our home PC. Whether it be assessing and choosing friends, spouses, vendors, or employees, we all fall victim to our human frailties and make errors in judgment. But let's face it: we don't typically conduct much due diligence before leaping to our decisions. We spend more time researching which car or cell phone to purchase than we do assessing a much more important and complex concept: human behavior and talent.

In our experience as researchers and human resources professionals, we see consistent patterns in companies that we can identify as the "deadly sins" of hiring, promoting, and developing the best and brightest.

1. **Inadequate Assessment:** Not spending enough time assessing the capability of the person or team before promoting or hiring that individual is a significant problem. We frequently see companies put senior hires through two or three 45-minute interviews about their job experiences, but they don't really find out what makes the potential hire tick. These types of interviews cannot possibly uncover the strengths and development needs of an individual and his or her ultimate fit in the organization. We call this type of

interviewing the "dating game." You date, but don't really get to know the person before you marry. Sometimes you find out that the life partner is not who you expected!

Making a mistake here is not only culturally costly, but economically a disaster. A mis-hire can cost more than 1.5 times their salary depending on the level of the role (Smart, 1999) A senior hire is an important hire. Many millions if not billions of dollars rest on this individual's ability and intellect. It is astonishing how little time is spent getting to know the potential hire and establishing what he or she can add to the enterprise.

In addition, top players prefer deep interviews and learning more about the company and the job as they are making a serious career decision for themselves (Smart, 1999).

Look for people who want to keep the date going for awhile. Remember, good dating is much less costly than a messy divorce, which will inevitably wreak havoc on the team and customers who rely on the team!

Here is a personal story about a company that did not use good interviewing techniques. After three interviews and the recruitment firm's recommendation, one candidate emerged as a star. After a deep assessment interview, it was discovered that the candidate did not have the titles and experience outlined in his resume, but rather had pulled out the skills he thought matched the job requirements and renamed his roles to fit the skills he believed the company wanted. This candidate made it to the finalist stage without being discovered. This is astonishing, but it is not all that uncommon.

Action: Build a strong hiring and recruiting process. Hold your search firms to the same rigor you use internally. Train your managers how to do talent assessment and support them with skilled human resource leaders who are equally trained.

2. **Using Faulty Assumptions:** In assessing potential new hires and promoting internal hires, we all too often make the following series of assessment assumptions that can lead to career crashes:

   Assumption 1: I know what this job is all about.
   Assumption 2: I know exactly what it takes to be a star in this job.
   Assumption 3: If I ask good questions, I'll figure out who is the best talent.
   Assumption 4: If I get a few other smart people involved in the interview, we will identify the best talent.

Assessment of the talent a job candidate may bring to an organization is challenging enough and these assumptions can lead to career crashes for the hiring manager as well as the new hire! *Action*: Ensure you have a clear definition of the job and what is needed to take the job to the next level. Clearly define the factors that are critical to success. Use multiple methods of assessment rather than relying on only one technique. (See chapter 6 appendix for steps that will help counter assessment assumptions and avoid career crashes.)

3. **Asking the Wrong Questions:** One of the most important lessons for assessment is to understand how your interview questions or other assessment tools link to the job being interviewed for. The assessor defines what good versus bad or match versus mismatch looks like for each interview probe or inventory score. We have often worked with managers who beam with pride when sharing their "sure bet" interview questions with us. You may be familiar with some of these yourself:

   "You are at a restaurant and the waiter brings you a steak cooked medium when you had ordered medium rare. What would you do?"

   Or these gems: "What sports did you play in high school and college?" "Did you grow up on a farm?"

   All of these questions are real. We know. We've heard them over and over again. These questions violate our assessment principles because they are not job-related and do not link to behaviors that would demonstrate either great or poor performance on the job. **Action:** Review the candidate's resume thoroughly. Think through the areas that need clarification and what needs to be probed. Write down the questions to be asked and be specific about what you are trying to learn. Avoid going off on tangents, which may be fun but shed no light on capability. Use a best-in-class profile to assess a candidate against with questions that align to that profile. (A sample of a best-in-class profile is in chapter 6 appendix.)

4. **Not Having Prepared Interviewers:** When getting multiple interviewers involved in the assessment process, make certain that they know the job requirements, success factors, and the interview protocol (including the definition of what a good or poor answer sounds like).

   Too often we find that a "strength-in-interviewer-numbers" approach is taken, only to learn that each interviewer asks the same or very similar questions and brings very different idiosyncratic methods for assessing the quality of a response.

Action: Take time up front to define what the work will be, the skills that will be needed to succeed, and the assessment methods that will best assess these skills. Getting everyone on the interview team aligned can be incredibly helpful in securing the best available talent.

5. **Not Assessing for Cultural Fit:** Will this individual fit into the organization's culture? Are you hiring them to change the current culture or support the one that is there? A classic error in hiring is not considering what type of environment an individual will thrive in and what type of environment could make an individual crash and burn.

   In our experience this is the most often overlooked area of hiring. It needs to be ferreted out in the assessment and interview process. When it comes to senior hires, rarely is the issue one of skill or question. Most people at this level have the requisite skills required if they have been successful in other companies. More frequently, it is the culture that causes the flameout. Candidates and interviewers alike often put their best foot forward only to find out that the organization does not value the same things as the new hire. This becomes a disaster for both parties. According to some executive search firms, the element of cultural fit is the biggest most significant derailer for external hires. Very few companies paint their culture as it really is when they are hiring talent. Like in the early days of dating, they appear as much as possible the way they think the candidate wants them to be. It is not until the candidate is on board that he or she sees the "real" company. Assessment clearly helps, because approaches and behaviors will become apparent to reveal whether a potential hire will or will not fit.

   Action: Know the behaviors that work and don't work in your culture. Use specific questions to probe for cultural fit. (See chapter 6 appendix for sample questions that highlight cultural fit. Remember, they need to be tailored to your unique culture.)

6. **Insufficient Onboarding:** Lots of people talk about onboarding, but few companies do an excellent job of onboarding outside hires or those who are being promoted. With an investment in good onboarding, you keep talent at their best and acclimate them to their new role. This ensures that they have time to accelerate their learning for success. Some say it's best to throw people into the new position—if they survive, great, if not, find someone else. What kind of message does this send to the rest of the work-

force, especially if these new hires have large parts of the business resting on their capabilities to learn and lead? It's not very good. A thorough assessment enables a clear onboarding action plan that assists the new hire in knowing what are red flags and what will help them be more successful.

Action: When hiring from the outside, the search firm should spend a fair amount of time helping the new hire understand the culture of the organization they are joining. The firm should also do a formal assessment of the behaviors the new hire has that will help him or her in the new company. If the new hire is part of a culture shift, he or she will meet tremendous resistance and will need an action plan to help navigate the new arena. This should be an automatic part of the hiring practice whether someone is being promoted from the inside or hired in from the outside. It is shocking how little of this is done by search firms today.

We recommend using the following model as a framework for an assessment (see Figure 6.2).

This model helps you look at candidates, whether for promotion or external hire, through four clear lenses. Quadrant 1 is job experience; Quadrant 2 is technical skills. Quadrant 3 is leadership skills. Quadrant 4 is cultural fit. Using these lenses ensures you get a full view of the person. Quadrants 1 and 2 are indicators of past experience and skills, and Quad-

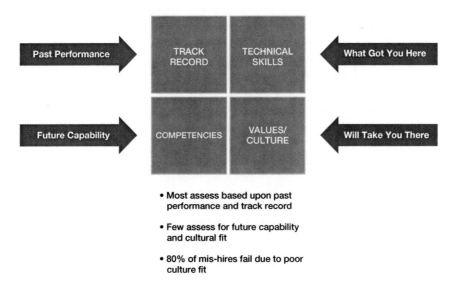

Figure 6.2 Framework for assessing talent.

rants 3 and 4 will help you understand the longer-term potential of a candidate. As an assessor you would develop questions for each of the quadrants and score the candidates against characteristics known to be those of top performers. In chapter 6 appendix, we have provided a sample interview guide based upon this four-quadrant model that is simple but guaranteed to provide true insight into potential candidates and talent. We would recommend that this guide be tailored to the unique requirements of your company and culture to make it a truly effective resource.

Getting Started: Building an Effective Assessment Practice

Here are our recommendations for building and implementing a successful assessment strategy:

Step One

As discussed in chapter 5, you should already have a clear understanding of your business strategy, especially as it links to people and performance. If you have not already done so, you must begin with clear answers to the following questions:

- What are your philosophy and strategy about talent and leadership?
- Do you believe that leadership is critical to the company's current and future success?
- Do you believe in developing talent internally or do you hire all senior leaders from the external marketplace?
- Do you have strong succession plans in place and do you know what your talent gaps are?

By answering these questions prior to launching your assessment protocols, you can ensure alignment between business strategies and human capital strategies.

Step Two

If you have not already done so, the next step is to define the characteristics of the leaders that you will need in the future. What is the profile that you believe will lead to your company's success?

Too often, companies have one set of leadership values that the senior executives talk about and another set of competencies that are used for executive assessment; or, there are complex competency models with layers and layers that no one understands. This adds unnecessary complexity to the topic of leadership and often confuses the leaders in the organization.

Step Three

Once you have developed the critical leadership competencies for success, it is essential to understand what those competencies look like when they are at their best and at their worst. This scale should be defined in visible and observable terms as it will give you a barometer against which to measure your executive and leadership talent.

Check out our sample assessment meter in chapter 6 appendix.

Step Four

Now it's time to develop your assessment methodology. It is critical to get this right the first time. A botched assessment cannot be rectified.

Follow this checklist to ensure you get off to a good start:

Assessment checklist

1. Define the **purpose** of the assessment process (talent identification, development, talent upgrading).
2. Decide **who** will be assessed: all executives, just your top talent, etc.
3. Determine **how** you will communicate the initiative to the organization. Is this about development only or performance feedback as well?
4. Identify **which** senior executives will serve as sponsors for the initiative.
5. Clarify the **methodologies** that will be used to conduct the assessments. Will you use an online 360 coupled with interviews, etc.?
6. Determine **what** the participants will receive—feedback report, coaching, etc.—and how these will be received. How will managers be engaged?
7. Clarify the **accountabilities**. What will the participant be required to do after receiving the assessment results (development planning accountabilities, training courses, etc.)? What will the manager be required to do and what support will be given?
8. Decide **who** will have access to the assessment data. Are there confidentiality issues?
9. Determine **what** follow-up you will provide and how you will track progress over time.
10. Agree on **who** will do the assessments. Will they be done internally, externally, or a combination of the two?

Step Five: Rigorously Communicate

It is of the utmost importance to communicate the assessment process in a straightforward, transparent manner. This will ensure that everyone involved in the assessment protocols understands how the data will be collected and used by the organization. It increases trust for the entire process.

Once the above is in place, you are ready to launch your strategy.

Assessment Outcomes

There are three levels of outcomes that can be leveraged effectively from a rigorous assessment strategy: the individual, the team or business unit, and the organization.

At the individual level, participants, perhaps for the first time, have clear, actionable feedback against which to develop a career plan or maybe an opportunity to speak with a coach to help construct a specific, development action plan. Additionally, individuals have an opportunity to understand what it will take for them to progress in their current organization and where they will need to invest personal time in order to prepare for possible promotions. This alone can be a significant step in retaining and engaging employees.

A recent exit-interview study conducted in a large conglomerate showed that employees who left the company voluntarily cited that the primary reason for their leaving was that they "were not clear on their career steps and had no career conversations." As one employee put it, "I did not think anyone cared about my career."

At the business unit or team level, a full assessment of leaders can show skills that are strengths and skills that are missing, but necessary, for the business strategy to succeed. This is powerful information because it makes clear what skills will need to be developed and what skills can be leveraged. For example, if a unit is trying to launch a new business line and it finds it lacks customer-related skills, it may have a difficult time getting traction.

At the organizational level, rigorous assessment data are perhaps at their most powerful. Here, one gets a total view of the characteristics of leaders who are successful in the current organization, and why some leaders who are successful today may need significant development in order to deliver results in the future. This view can help you readily identify cross-organizational development needs and make swift talent decisions. This can be a huge eye-opener.

These assessments reveal which types of behaviors and skills will do best in which circumstances, and if your performance management systems and other feedback mechanisms align and reinforce the behaviors and skills you require. You begin to get a clear picture of what type of culture your company values. You may or may not like the picture, but it gives you a baseline against which to drive change and measure improvement.

Here is an example of what we mean. A company did a thorough assessment of its leaders and found that the skills least valued and rewarded in leaders were their people-development and team-building skills. Yet the company continually voiced in slogans and recruitment materials that this was a place to develop and grow. Clearly it was not! Conducting assessments, tracking, and statistically validating results can be leading indicators of the overall health of your workforce.

Results that Matter

Having done a thorough assessment of your talent, you are now ready to implement the rest of your talent optimization plan. You know what skills need to be developed and for whom. You can clearly segment your talent by skills. You can take regional deep dives and functional deep dives. You have the ability to customize your talent tactics to focus on elements that will raise the quality of the existing talent. You know who your stars are and what they do specifically that makes them stars.

This gives you an outstanding profile of the types of individuals who succeed in your company. Once you have this profile, you have your template for success. Assessment provides the hardcore analytics that should drive every talent system. It takes the guesswork out of hiring, developing, promoting, and giving feedback to your talent. How many times have you heard from employees that they do not get enough feedback and how many times have you heard from managers that they hate delivering bad performance feedback news and struggle articulating the behaviors that will help an employee move forward? Assessments ensure that the messages about what someone does well and what they need to improve are clear.

Another result of talent assessments is that your training dollars will be spent primarily on those skills most correlated with executive success. Development plans can be designed to be specific, tailored, and relevant for each executive. New assignments and job rotations can be identified to systematically provide executives with the experiences and exposures they need in order to hasten development and add value to the company. Clear talent road maps can be put in place to drive actions that are measurable and can be tracked to show progress from the initial assessment baseline to your ideal state.

Again, a forward-looking assessment, if done well, can reduce your executive search costs, increase retention rate for new hires, and ensure that you have a succession pool ready to move into open positions, reducing "time-to-fill" significantly.

All of these steps take costs out of your human capital operation and add value to your company's game plan for winning the "war for talent." So, what are you waiting for? The investment in assessment can be a significant game changer and cost reducer, while also giving you the tools to engage your workforce at a time when it is important to keep your talent—and enhance that talent after the upturn. Now is the time to invest. But invest smartly and in the right things—the things that position you to win the "war for talent."

Once you have aligned your leaders and culture, built your talent strategy around your business strategy, and done a deep-dive assessment of your talent, you are ready to go! You now know:

- Who you have to develop and in what areas,
- The types of people you need to hire and what they look like,
- Who is ready for promotion and into what roles,
- The specific feedback that each individual will be receiving,
- Who your stars are (which you can now prove not just with business results),
- The defensible information on the potential of your talent for your company's overall talent review process.

But perhaps most importantly, you have the baseline against which to measure progress and show tangible results that can be directly correlated to the performance of the company—something very few organizations do when it comes to people.

References

Smart, B. D. (1999). *Topgrading: How leading companies win by hiring, coaching and keeping the best people.* Upper Saddle River, NJ: Prentice Hall.

Wheeler, P. (2010). Making successful transitions: The leader's perspective. In M. Goldsmith, J. Baldoni, & S. McArthur. (Eds.). *The AMA handbook of leadership* (pp. 187–202). New York: AMACOM.

APPENDIX 6:
TALENT SCORECARD

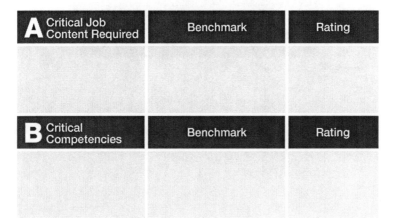

1 EXPERIENCE

	Minimal Experience	Significant Experience
Business Cycles		✔
Customer Types/ Size & Complexity		✔
Job Roles		✔
Regions & Cultures	✔	

2 LEADERSHIP FACTORS

QUARTERLIES

	Bottom	2nd	3rd	Top
Results Focus			■	
Customer Focus			■	
Business Focus		■		
Team Focus	■			

Quartile comparisons are based on an external database of high-performing executives and senior leaders.

3 DETAILED COMPETENCY PROFILE

RESULTS FOCUS
- Self-Starter
- Assertiveness
- Results Accountability
- Project Planning
- Line of Sight

CUSTOMER FOCUS
- Service Responsiveness
- Global Perspective
- Develop Innovative Solutions

BUSINESS FOCUS
- Financial Acumen
- Analyzing & Diagnosis
- Decisiveness
- Strategic Planning
- Risk Taking
- Accelerating Change

TEAM FOCUS
- Relationship Building
- Listening & Receptivity
- Teamwork
- Influencing
- Motivating
- Developing Talent
- Self-Development

1 2 3 4 5 6 7

PERFORMANCE LEVELS
1. Strong Development Need
2. Development Need
3. Opportunity for Growth
4. Solid Evidence
5. Strength to Leverage
6. Excellent Strength to Leverage
7. Outstanding Strength to Leverage

JOB ANALYSIS TOOL

A Critical Job Content Required	Benchmark	Rating
B Critical Competencies	Benchmark	Rating

Ensure job requirements are aligned to future needs

SAMPLE ASSESSMENT METER

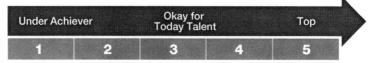

Under Achiever	Okay for Today Talent	Top
1	**2**	**3**	**4**	**5**

Service
Orientation

Adaptability

TRACK RECORD

WHAT TO ASK	WHAT TO LISTEN FOR
• What did you enjoy least/most in the role? • What major challenges did you face? • What mistakes did you make and what did you learn from them? • What did your boss see as your major strengths/weaknesses? • What has been your performance on key deliverables? • What did you do to take your job to the next level?	• Do their likes and dislikes fit with your role? • Are the challenges similar to your role? • Could they admit mistakes? • Are they self-aware? • Could they move the needle to build a better organization? • Could they lead through adversity?

RED FLAGS

• Can't articulate any mistakes or development needs
• Personality self-unaware
• Difficulty performing in tough times
• Making excuses, defensive

TECHNICAL SKILLS

WHAT TO ASK

- What is your strongest technical skill?
- What is the technical skill that you use the least or are least comfortable with?
- How do you pick up new technical skills?
- What do you see as the biggest market trends in your field and why?
- What are you doing to stay abreast of these trends?
- Who are your biggest competitors, what are their offerings and solutions and how will that impact this role?

WHAT TO LISTEN FOR

- Do strengths fit your needs?
- Are their deficiencies critical requirements?
- Do they seek out new skills?
- Do they apply the new skills?
- Do they understand the market conditions?
- Are they attuned to competitors?

RED FLAGS

- Learn but don't act
- Academic or superficial answers
- Do not adapt well to new methods/approaches

PEOPLE LEADERSHIP

WHAT TO ASK

- Are you a natural leader and if so, cite indications?
- Give an example of when someone followed your lead and when they did not.
- What happens when people fail to perform? What do you do?
- What type of performance management system do you use?
- How do you develop your teams?
- Can you give me an example of how you give feedback?
- How would your subordinates describe your approaches to training and development?

WHAT TO LISTEN FOR

- Do they have a clear sense of leadership?
- Do they believe in developing others?
- Do they use feedback as an effective tool?
- Can they make tough calls?
- Do they give credit to others?

RED FLAGS

- Micro-management tendencies
- Don't believe in people development
- Very tactical
- Accept mediocrity

ORGANIZATION VALUES

WHAT TO ASK

- What was the culture like at your previous organization?
- What did you like about the culture and what did you not like?
- How did you deal with the aspects you didn't like?
- Describe the culture in which you thrive.
- Describe a situation where there was an intense pressure to compromise your integrity.
- Describe a courageous action or unpopular position you have taken.

WHAT TO LISTEN FOR

- Elements that don't fit with organization values
- Any integrity issues – hedging
- How they interact with others – teamwork
- Courage and guts under pressure

RED FLAGS

- Blames others
- Is indecisive – won't take a stand
- Avoids conflict

PROFILE OF A "BEST-IN-CLASS LEADER"

TRACK RECORD

- Deep knowledge of industry, customers, and competitors and uses it to advantage
- Consistently beats goals
- Successfully worked through tough challenges
- Self aware – constantly tries to improve
- Leaves behind a sustainable organization

ORGANIZATIONAL COMPETENCIES

- Develops people consistently
- Cares about people
- Is future oriented
- Deals well with complexity
- Fosters open dialogue
- Shares wins and successes
- Knows how to get things done

TECHNICAL SKILLS

- Deep domain knowledge
- Unique knowledge of field
- Always seeks out new information/skills in field
- Anticipates future trends and acts on them
- Picks up technical things quickly

ORGANIZATIONAL VALUES

- Takes responsibility for own actions
- Treats people with respect
- Understands own development needs
- Takes risks/does the right thing in face of pressure

CHAPTER 7

PERFORMANCE MANAGEMENT
The Fallacy of the Current Systems

Optimizing Talent, pages 85–96
Copyright © 2011 by Information Age Publishing

How Do You Know If You Have It Right?

Years ago, Dr. Edward Deming advocated the removal of barriers that rob hourly workers and people in management of their pride of workmanship. Among other things, "This implies the abolition of the annual merit rating system (performance appraisals) and of management by objective. Again, the responsibility of managers, supervisors, and foremen must be changed from sheer numbers to quality." When asked what should replace performance appraisals in the workplace, Dr. Deming (1982) said simply, "Try leadership."

Performance management systems as they are currently constructed do not work. Why organizations spend time and money on such a demoralizing system is beyond us. Regular feedback and being clear about what is expected are far more powerful than having an elaborate form and technology system that is completed once a year. These systems do not create meaningful dialogue and focus. So why do we spend so much time on these antiquated performance management systems?

Some would argue that lawyers and litigious employees have gotten the best of us. Of course, there are litigious employees and there are managers who act inappropriately and don't know how to effectively supervise and manage employees. But, as in any bell curve, litigious employees are not the majority. Elaborate systems have been put in place to deal with the minority, rather than energize and motivate the majority. Significant time is spent assembling systems that have boxes to check to document that managers have, in fact, had performance discussions with their employees, that goals have been set, that employees and managers have reviewed them, and so on. There is no end to the ingenious methods created to ensure that managers have at least one conversation with their employees relative to their employees' performance per year. As with many of the tactics and tools initiated by lawyers and human resources professionals, managers fail to see the day-to-day value of these exercises. Employees fail to see the value as well.

The primary reasons that performance management systems are seen as cumbersome, non-value adds are that they:

- Are poorly executed. For instance, we know of companies that give very short windows for managers to write the appraisals and have the review discussions;
- Provide limited valuable feedback about what is done well and what needs improvements;
- Are not timely.

Performance discussions are frequently tied to compensation discussions, so employees are much more focused on the possible bonus or increase and have little interest in the feedback. In fact, according to the research conducted by leading expert on engagement Beverly Kaye (Kaye and Jordan-Evans, 2008), many employees view their bonus or salary increase as feedback since they generally receive little verbal feedback on how they are doing throughout the year. The manager, on the other hand, can't wait for the experience to be over, especially if there is some bad news to deliver. When pinned down for reasons why the review was not what the employee expected, they will blame it on others, saying something like, "Others have not seen good performance." How many times have you used or experienced the phrase, "I would have loved to have given you a better review, but my boss wouldn't let me," or another classic, "You know, we use a distribution curve and I had to give some people a poorer rating than others; if it were up to me I would have rated you higher." Another often-heard rationale is, "If I give this employee a bad rating she won't be able to move to another part of the company." These are all just excuses for not wanting or knowing how to have meaningful discussions with employees on how they can continue to grow in their roles.

The coup de grâce is that managers and employees often view the experience as a onetime shot for giving negative or, as some would say, "constructive," feedback, even if the employee's performance has been relatively good.

What we have described above is what we call the "performance management syndrome." To spot this syndrome quickly and easily, look for the following characteristics:

1. *The purpose of the performance management system is not clear and companies have lost sight of it.* The organization does not recognize or put emphasis on the fact that the purpose of a performance management system is to A) provide feedback and coaching so that employees can be more effective on the job, B) give recognition to employees for achieving goals effectively, and C) ensure alignment to the overall goals of the enterprise. It is at least one method managers should use to determine who are the stars and best performers, which employees may not be pulling their weight, and how all employees might better meet the goals of the organization.

2. *Too much focus is placed on getting the ratings right and too much time is spent on the scale and the definitions.* One organization we know of actually went out and polled managers as to whether they wanted

to use numbers or letters for the rating scale. They then debated for weeks about which one they would use. Everyone was fixated on the ratings rather than on the content of the discussion. Another company spent hours deciding whether someone should be rated a 3.3 or a 3.5 on a 5-point scale. The problem with a mid-line rating is that only those who are rated highly will be satisfied with the system. It is very hard for anyone to feel good about being rated average. Ratings, at best are distracting. According to Professor Donald Mitchell (2001), you need to free people up to feel good about themselves, to become better, and to cooperate to improve the organization. People's value and importance cannot be reduced to a number. Way too much time is spent in the "command-and-control" mode—monitoring, evaluating, and judging people.

3. *In most cases, performance management systems are hardwired to compensation and that becomes the overriding factor.* Discussing career aspirations is usually overlooked. In reviewing exit-interview data from several companies, one of the biggest reasons that employees leave is because they have no line of sight to their next career move. In *The 2020 Workplace,* Jeanne C. Meister and Karie Willyerd (2010) predict that at least one big workforce trend will be employees evaluating employers to ensure that their career aspirations can be met in the organization and that there is a match with where they see themselves and where the company sees them. Critical to this discussion is providing the guidance and support that enable employees to increase their capabilities and their ability to keep up with emerging trends.

4. *Many systems focus solely on the achievement of work goals to the exclusion of how these goals are achieved.* The fact that the leader may have left a pile of dead bodies or demoralized employees as a result of achieving his or her goals is not factored into the equation. Assessment of leadership and interpersonal skills needs to be included in the discussion. This assessment should also be aligned to the values of the company. We have spent a lot of time discussing the virtues of being clear on leadership expectations, having a leadership framework that is aligned to the organization's strategy and values, and being able to assess talent to determine strengths and improvement needs. These factors must be articulated and reinforced in performance discussions so that employees can see what they need to improve in order to move forward in their careers and advance the organization.

5. *The performance system is disconnected from the overall business strategy and objectives and linked solely to the siloed goals of a department or unit.* First and foremost, for companies to achieve high performance, they must have employees working on projects and issues that matter most to the enterprise. Without goal alignment to the business strategy, this cannot happen. Employees focus on their own goals when they don't understand how the whole company works. Here is a classic example of what happens when the leadership team is not aligned around goals. We witnessed a team of leaders who actually groaned at the thought of having goals that supported each other and the overall focus of the company. While this team agreed to set goals to support the business and not just their silo, the sidebar conversation as they were leaving the room was, "My team is going to work on what I think is important so I can make my numbers. I don't care about the rest of the organization." As intellectually evident it is that goals should be aligned, it is shocking how few organizations achieve goal alignment and hold their leaders accountable to take action for the greater good of the whole organization.

Performance management systems certainly have their place in an overall approach to developing people. However, they have been overrated in their impact on performance and bottom-line results. Deming himself would say that it is important to measure and provide feedback accurately to employees, but in an "adult-to-adult" context.

Our study shows that of all the levers for ensuring that the organization has the best talent, the performance management system, while important, has the smallest impact on business outcomes and results. The startling finding is that most organizations spend an inordinate amount of time "perfecting" this system to the exclusion of all others. Other than the legal implications when companies want to get rid of or lay off employees, we are not sure why this is. Significant time and energy are put into making sure these systems are online and that the employee and manager discussion is captured and recorded.

If you ask, most managers would tell you that performance management systems are designed to help them give employees feedback so that they can do better jobs. However, most employees will tell you that the system is ineffective for this purpose. How do we know? Read employee satisfaction surveys: the areas that are most often lower-scoring items are "My manager gives me the feedback I need to do my job better," and "I get the feedback I need to improve."

Looking at these issues from the manager's point of view, many managers struggle with delivering less-than-satisfactory reviews. They don't know how to give effective feedback and coaching. In interviews with senior human resources professionals, we found they are still looking for ways to equip managers to deliver negative feedback and to have difficult conversations. We think it is distressing that managers have to spend time giving negative feedback. Performance feedback is supposed to help people get better, not demoralize them about what they did wrong. This is Deming's primary criticism of performance management systems. It is much easier to critique errors committed in the past than to give constructive coaching that will help someone see where they are doing things right and how they could do something better. According to Tom Coens and Mary Jenkins in *Abolishing Performance Appraisals* (2002), coaching and development conversations are much more powerful than criticism as they motivate and encourage people based on what they are doing right.

Daniel Pink's (2009) most recent work also underscores the above points. He argues that, to be more effective, employees want coaching and feedback that helps them get better. They want goals that are aspirational and achievable. They want to know when they are doing something right so they can replicate it.

The following case study illustrates these arguments by contrasting a critical, negative approach with one that is more positive and motivational. In a seminar run by Human Synergistics, a challenge was put to a room of very successful leaders. Half the room received feedback on what was done wrong and the other half received feedback on what was done right. Each group was then given another similar problem and asked to solve it. The part of the room that received the negative feedback struggled with how to solve the puzzle. At least half of the group that had received negative feedback did not solve the problem and those who did took a considerable amount of time to do so. The part of the room that had initially received positive feedback solved the problem in record time and most of the teams got the right answer!

Performance management systems have their place, but the mechanical system that most organizations seem to rely on should be the last step in an ongoing yearly process to ensure that employees are getting the coaching and appropriate feedback they need to be successful. Coaching employees to be successful should be part of every manager's job. The coaching should be clear, specific, and timely, not a Pavlovian carrot-and-stick approach.

What happens when you use the Pavlovian approach? Take dog training: when the dog does something good, the trainer tells him, "Good job."

(How many times do you hear that around the workplace? Because the manager is not specific as to what was done well, how does the employee ensure that he or she can do it again?) The dog then gets a treat (sort of like a bonus). This pattern continues and soon the dog expects a treat every time it does something "good." After a short while of not receiving a treat, the dog reverts back to its original habits or becomes dysfunctional. It is the same with employee bonuses. If we get a reward or an increase for a "good job," then whenever we do a good job we expect the reward. It creates entitlement, so if we don't get the bonus or it goes to someone else, we become de-motivated.

Compensation is not a long-term motivator. It creates short-term satisfaction and can send the wrong messages, especially if management is not clear about the behaviors that were associated with it. As Steve Kerr points out in his recent book *Reward System: Does Yours Measure Up?* (2008), "You get what you pay for," so be very careful about what you reward and don't. Additionally, because an organization can't continuously provide bonuses and not everyone receives the same amount anyway, the system frequently becomes a de-motivator. According to a study done by Deloitte (2010), greater compensation is not enough to keep an employee satisfied. Innovation is the key motivator and being on the cutting-edge is far more satisfying. This study also found that performance was lowest in the highest bonus-structure jobs both internationally and in the US.

Let's look at two case studies to exemplify this point. In Company A, the performance management system is set up to provide three discussions: 1) how employees perform against the business goals; 2) how they behave according to the values and leadership requirements, i.e., what their strengths and weaknesses are and what they need to work on in order to move forward in their career; and 3) what are each employee's career aspirations and how do they sync up with what the manager sees as realistic career goals for each person in the company? Conversations take at least an hour and there is good dialogue. Employees feel as though the manager understands their career goals, is trying to help them achieve those goals, and discusses things they have to do to achieve their goals, as well as how they will be supported in their careers. This is a good performance discussion. The flaw, however, is that it only occurs once or twice a year. This discussion is positive, motivational, and it builds trust between manager and employee; it's just not enough. (See chapter 7 appendix.)

Company B, on the other hand, is interested in speed. Its goal is to get the performance review and compensation discussions into one session as quickly as possible. This fact speaks volumes about what the company culture values: speed. Little time is spent on the human dimension of development or on employees' personal career aspirations. The employee surveys reveal that everyone had a performance review with his or her manager. The company applauded itself for such great scores. However, the question of whether or not the discussion was meaningful was never asked. A company we worked with did something similar with its customer surveys. Time and again, it surveyed its customers and received very high marks each time. However, customer retention was very low. When asked why they left for competitors, customers responded that the questions on the survey were about things important to the organization, not to the customers. So they may have appeared satisfied, but that was because the right questions were not being asked. The same holds true with performance discussions and coaching. Those at the top have an obligation to find out what is important to their employees and how they can help them achieve their goals.

Which company in the examples above do you think had the higher retention rate? You guessed it, Company A. Though infrequent, meaningful dialogue and career discussions helped Company A increase its managers' connection with employees, so the employees felt someone cared about them and their careers. As mentioned in chapter 6, a company did a study of why talent was leaving the organization. The prevailing reason put on anonymous exit-interview surveys was that there were no career discussions with employees, which meant employees did not have a "line of sight" to their next role or longer-term career aspirations.

Here is what a company could do to ensure that performance management has the desired effect. Company C's managers have been trained to give effective coaching to their employees. Managers set goals jointly in a dialogue with their teams, and team members share their goals collectively with each other so they can see the alignment of what they are doing. The teams and managers talk about how they are going to move their goals forward and what might be some contingencies in the plan. Each month, team members review their progress together and ask each other for feedback and ideas about the technical aspects of the project and how to improve on an interpersonal skill level. Managers meet regularly with individual team members and ask how they think they are doing, what help they need to continue, the obstacles they are facing, and how managers can help.

Managers also use data from the individual assessments (discussed in chapter 6). They make sure there is alignment between the assessment feedback, strengths, and development needs, and that which is discussed in the performance cycle. Managers use this data to offer coaching that is focused on the future plans and actions to be taken and give some developmental coaching to help guide the employee. The discussion is a true give and take. Lots of listening and relevant questioning on the part of managers and employees are exhibited in the meetings. Periodic checks-in are conducted—no painful pitches are presented for review and critique by managers. Both employees and managers engage in regular dialogue. In this way, managers, employees, and teams can gauge their performance and how well they are achieving their respective goals so that at the end of the performance cycle, there will be no surprises. The performance results are clear throughout the year. The cycle repeats with a reflection on lessons learned, successes achieved, and celebration for work well done or corrections for the future. Goals are set, strengths and development areas are discussed, and career aspirations are revisited. This is the scenario of a world-class performance management system that is repeatable, consistent, reliable, and positive for all—even those who have performance issues that need to be addressed.

So what is the antidote to the performance management syndrome?

In the best of all worlds we would go back to Deming and "bag" many of the complicated performance review systems that exist today. Performance management should be an ongoing process in an organization in which talent is getting regular coaching with frequent discussions about their goals, measures of success, and how they are achieving their goals. If this can't be done, here is what you do. Follow these 12 steps to build a performance-rich organization.

12 Steps to a Performance-Rich Organization

1. Ensure that your performance system has three components: 1) job-related goals, 2) goals that support organizational values, and 3) behavioral strengths and improvement areas that support personal growth and career aspirations.
2. Keep the system simple—no lengthy reports. Our preference would be to see only a one- or two-page document. We've included our preferred tool in chapter 7 appendix.
3. Be clear about the leadership behavior required in the company. Ensure that everyone gets feedback on how they are progressing on the leadership aspects of their roles. Ensure that the feedback is aligned with the individual assessments described in chapter 6.
4. The system should focus on the best-in-class profile for a particular job or function and provide for discussions about how an employee can achieve that profile.

5. Ensure that leaders are trained to give coaching and effective behavioral feedback. Make sure that leaders know it is their job to ensure employees have effective coaching.
6. Select a consistent model for coaching and apply it throughout the organization. Ensure that those coaching are skilled in the model.
7. Educate leaders about how to have career discussions with employees and provide career paths with the required skills clearly delineated, so that employees and managers can envision a future path that is realistic.
8. Create a culture where it is okay to ask for feedback: Teach employees how to coach each other. Use peer-coaching models and build cohorts or learning circles, so teams can learn from each other how to effectively address an issue or apply a best practice.
9. Leverage social media to enable learning and feedback exchange.
10. Measure the effectiveness of your approach through employee satisfaction surveys. Ensure that the questions directly relate to the above components.
11. Catch people doing things right: Reinforce the behaviors required for business success.
12. Have frequent celebrations for building capability: Recognize and celebrate growth.

Finally, ask yourself the following questions and assess how your employees would answer them. Evaluate yourself. Don't rely on a system to ensure that people are getting what they need to be successful and create organization value.

1. Are you specific about and do you reinforce what people are doing right?
2. Are you approachable for questions and advice?
3. Do you encourage your team members to help each other improve?
4. Do you make it okay to ask questions in group settings?
5. Do you offer clear and specific examples of best practices and encourage others to share best practices?
6. Do you encourage your team members to explore development opportunities?
7. Do you know the personal career aspirations of each of your direct reports?

If you can't answer yes to all of these questions, then you have some work to do. Don't feel bad, you are not alone!

References

Coens, T., & Jenkins, M. (2002). *Abolishing performance appraisals: Why they backfire and what to do instead.* San Francisco: Berrett-Kohler.

Deloitte Consulting, LLP. (2010, April). *Has the great recession changed the talent game? Six guideposts to managing talent out of a turbulent economy.* Retrieved September 9, 2010 from http://www.deloitte.com/assets/Dcom-Austria/Local%20Assets/Documents/HCAS/Talent%20Management/at_TalentPulseWrap.pdf

Deming, W. E. (1982). *Out of Crisis* (9th printing). Cambridge, MA: MIT Press.

Kaye, B., & Jordan-Evans, S. (2008). *Love 'em or lose 'em: Getting good people to stay* (4th ed.). San Francisco: Berrett-Koehler Publishers.

Kerr, S. (2008). *Reward systems: Does yours measure up?* MA: Harvard Business School Press.

Meister, J. C., & Willyerd, K. (2010). *The 2020 workplace: How innovative companies attract, develop, and keep tomorrow's employees today.* New York: HarperCollins.

Mitchell, D. (2001). Abolish bureaucracy to encourage movement. [Review of the book *Abolishing performance appraisals: Why they backfire and what to do instead*]. Retrieved September 9, 2010 from http://www.bkconnection.com/ProdDetails.asp?ID=1576752003

Pink, D. (2009). *Drive: The surprising truth about what motivates us.* New York: Riverhead Books.

APPENDIX 7:
SAMPLE PERFORMANCE REVIEW FORM

Employee _____ **Manager** _____

Accomplishments: Please provide your key accomplishments for the year and the impact they had on your group and the company.

Development: Please list your 3 or 4 key strengths and development areas.

STRENGTHS	DEVELOPMENT

Aspirations: What are your career goal for the next 3 to 5 years?

Action Plan: List 2 to 3 things you will do this year to continue to build skills toward your career goals.

CHAPTER 8

LEARNING AND DEVELOPMENT
Maximizing the Talent Pool

Optimizing Talent, pages 97–109
Copyright © 2011 by Information Age Publishing
All rights of reproduction in any form reserved.

How most of us intend to develop the talents and abilities of our team members is a far cry from the medieval methods that we often use. Our intuition and common sense tell us that people are important and that the key to our success as managers is inextricably linked to the talents and skills of our team members. Then why do the development methods we use so often look more like torture than nurture? We'll get to that a bit later. First, having interviewed more than 20,000 leaders about their approaches to talent development, we have surfaced many less-than-ideal practices that you may recognize.

Talent Destruction Practices

The "Hide and Seek" Game: (aka "How to Snuff out Your Talent")

This game goes a little like this. A talented performer overachieves. He/she shows a great deal of motivation, commitment, and skills; makes wonderful contributions; and, like most high achievers, seeks advancement and growth. Our shrewd manager knows a good thing when she sees it. If she can keep this person on her team, she thinks she can get more done and look like a star herself. Simple, pragmatic, and brilliant, right? Unfortunately not. As our manager hides the talents of this wonderful team member, a funny thing happens. The employee's talents begin to hide as well. Less engaged, feeling a bit trapped and unappreciated, our once-rising star is closer to resignation.

Our research confirmed that organizations with managers who share talent, cross-promote successes within departments, shine the light on talented individuals, and provide new challenges to such employees are much more successful than organizations with managers who play the "Hide and Seek" game. In fact, a very smart leader of a top outsourcing organization said, "We take pride in seeding talent in other organizations. First, we have a friend in another company (this makes good business sense), and we get a reputation for developing great leaders."

The "Buried Alive" Test (aka "Let's See If You Can Survive")

Many of us have fallen prey to this next destructive development practice. The boss is piling work up on us. We can barely see over the piles of projects on our desks, and our email inbox is approaching the point of "no reply." We recognize that we are buried with no time to devote to coaching our people. Then in a moment of inspired empowerment, we shovel huge amounts of the work over to our already overwhelmed team members. We think to ourselves, "What a wonderful development opportunity for these people. Let's see who can swim and who cannot!"

Our study of good practices for development does acknowledge that *stretch assignments* (giving a talented person a bit more than they think they can handle) is one appropriate tool for development. However, if it is the only tool in the development shed, there will be a problem. The "Buried Alive" method leads to burnout, and ultimately, turnover: talented people leave or give up because they just can't keep up.

Organizations and managers who excel at talent development consistently take a proactive approach. They identify specific activities and practice opportunities for their people. They have serious career development discussions that, as noted in chapter 7, take into account the aspirations of their employees as well as the needs of the company. Smart companies think ahead several jobs for employees and don't just hire them or promote them for the job at hand. These managers think about the assignments not only from the perspective of delivering on business outcomes, but also from the perspective of what the developmental experience will provide to the employee. To be successful, this requires thinking ahead, planning, dialogue, skill and development needs assessment, and coaching. You are probably starting to see some common themes emerge: You can't avoid practices like career development and planning, coaching, and assessment. They are critical to developing your talent. Additionally, our research underscores their powerful link to business outcomes.

The "Public Flogging" Lesson (aka "You Are Never Good Enough")

In any learning environment, research shows us that feedback is a necessary component. However, for many of us, the feedback we provide too often has the opposite impact of what we expected. How many times have you been on the giving or receiving end of negative feedback concerning performance?

Many managers have the uncanny ability to find flaws in everything and everyone. Compounding the impact of this ability is the direct communication style such managers use to call out these flaws in team settings. These managers are probably working under the assumption that a "harsh stick" is a wonderful learning tool. They may have a subconscious memory of their mothers shouting at them as young children, "You idiot! Don't touch the stove. It's hot!" or as young adults when reviewing school report cards, "What is the matter with you dummy? Couldn't you turn those A minuses into real A's?"

In any event, while studies have shown that, for a very short amount of time, negative reinforcement and feedback can improve performance, this is a recipe for talent decline and escape when relied upon as a consistent development tool. Most managers with whom we have talked rely on this technique most often when they themselves are feeling like failures and receiving negative feedback from their managers. This is a cascading, self-fulfilling problem. And guess what, it gets louder and harsher the further down in the organization it goes. Combine this flogging with tight time frames to deliver and you are creating an organization that will be fraught with unintentional integrity issues. People will cover up their mistakes, blame others for their errors, and ultimately leave in frustrated exhaustion.

Our study clearly reinforces that having a feedback-rich environment is a critical component in keeping highly talented people engaged and thriving. Managers who have consistent career development discussions with their people have much higher workforce motivation and engagement. Some of our key findings regarding feedback confirm that it should be:

1. Frequent and balanced
2. Focused on leveraging strengths and developing weaknesses
3. Aligned to the career aspirations of the individual
4. Future-focused, i.e., based on *FeedForward* (Goldsmith, 2002)[1] as an organizational competency.

Using these four principles of feedback ensures real on-the-job learning and development. Teaching your teams to use these principles creates a learning-rich culture.

"Be Like Me" Mentoring (aka "My Way or the Highway")

In our well-intentioned quest to create an entire empire of "mini-me's," we often teach as we would like to be taught. That is why our studies of executive teams typically find similar patterns of values, behaviors, and leadership styles commonplace across teams. When consulting with senior leaders about the make-up of talent in their organizations, a favorite line we hear is, "Well, Mr. President, the apple does not fall far from the tree." This means both good habits and bad habits. In today's fluid, fast-changing business environment, that type of leadership homogeneity can make it difficult for an organization or a team to shift gears quickly enough to meet the evolv-

---

1. The purpose of Feed*Forward* is to provide individuals, teams, and organizations with suggestions for the future and to help them achieve a positive change in behavior.

ing needs of the marketplace. Groupthink sets in and no new ideas or innovations come into play, because everyone is thinking alike and usually congratulating themselves on how good their thoughts are. Unfortunately, the rest of the world is not that homogeneous. Jim Collins (2009) would say that lack of diversity of thought and having groupthink are key factors contributing to the death spiral of organizations. This type of homogeneity creates cultures that cannot innovate, because leaders see the problem through restricted lenses. Additionally, when a new person with fresh ideas is hired (usually using the poor hiring practices that we have discussed earlier), the organization antibodies set in and "kill" the new ideas. The dejected, smart, talented individual will likely stick it out for awhile, but ultimately he or she will leave for more accepting pastures.

Our research indicates that the best talent organizations place an overt value on diversity—of backgrounds, skill sets, thinking, and viewpoints. Diversity of thought is considered a critical competitive advantage for these organizations. The best teams look for talent that will bring a new, fresh, and divergent lens to the discussion, rather than having a room full of "mini-me's." We also see that leaders who value diversity of thought have the most diverse teams culturally. These leaders don't need to go to awareness seminars to help them see the "business case" for diversity. They know it is critical to their success for future growth, and they have a leadership style that supports diverse thinking. They listen, facilitate dialogue, and have open, transparent discussions; they encourage constructive debate to come up with the best solution. As discussed earlier, the prevailing leadership style in most organizations is command-and-control, so we don't see a lot of those behaviors out there. But as you read this and say to yourself, "Of course, this makes sense," why not take the next step and apply it?

The "Never Look Up" Trap (aka "Keep Your Head in the Sand")

As leaders, we often put people in imaginary boxes. We value what they have done and the tasks they have mastered, so we give them more of the same. What often happens is that a high-potential employee becomes typecast for what he or she can do better than anyone else on the team, rather than being given opportunities to look up from their tactical work to gain experiences in new and unchartered territories.

We have worked with organizations in which all of the high potentials possess the same basic skill set. They are driven, accountable, project implementers who have an uncanny ability to respond to the needs of their customers. They are managers and not leaders. In discussing career progression with these high potentials, we hear the same story over and over again. It goes something like this:

"I am very good at what I do. The organization relies on me to execute my projects. As I get faster and better at executing my projects, I am given more of the same projects to complete in an even shorter time frame with fewer resources. I know I am weak in leadership areas that have to do with strategy creation, business acumen, leading change, and building teams, but I haven't had any exposure to doing any of these things."

The outcome of this scenario is that people do not develop enough to take bigger jobs that require more leadership and strategic thinking. When the company finally realizes that they need more than just execution skills, their talent is so entrenched that they can no longer stretch to new business requirements or changing customer demands. This is a sad scenario, especially for people in the latter parts of their careers who are let go because their skill sets are no longer relevant. They were great for the job as it was, but not for the future growth.

Our research indicates that organizations that focus on and encourage broader leadership skills get branded in the marketplace as places to develop terrific talent. We have found that this branding is directly correlated with achieving strong business results. Our friend who is COO for a large company puts it this way: "We don't have to advertise our brand and how we lead; our customers do it for us. We are transparent around how we make decisions, open about our talent and the mistakes we've made, and honest about how we learn from each other and our customers how to fix our mistakes. We are never static in our approach. We are always trying to learn how to do things better to meet changing customer needs." This statement reflects how companies create learning organizations.

Coaching is a critical element in a learning organization. And, as noted before, in our research we found that coaching is hardwired to results. This is one skill set required by leaders that will not be going away anytime soon. In fact, though it has been around since the time of Socrates, many of us aren't any good at it.

Now that we have alerted you to several talent destroyers, we will turn our attention to what every leader needs to know about making talent development a clear advantage.

Making Talent Development a Clear Advantage

Most organizations financially support leadership development and training. Over the past decade, we have seen organizations shift from a classroom training philosophy to multi-method approaches that combine experiential learning and distance learning with classroom training. These advances in the delivery of learning solutions have made a positive impact on leadership development. They have allowed individuals greater learning opportunities and provided a more relevant connection between what they are learning and how they can apply and practice their new skills and behaviors on the job.

Within the Talent Optimization Framework and Survey™, learning and development typically receives scores in the mid-range. It should be considered a "work-in-progress" area. While most companies highlight successes in this area, they also point out how things can still be improved.

As revealed in our survey, areas in which organizations seem to be making great strides include "Learning and development is easily available to all within the organization" and "Learning and development makes use of multiple methods to accommodate diverse learning styles (e.g., job assignments, coaches, mentors, classroom training, etc.)." We are seeing a much higher frequency of technology-enabled training provided to employees as well as an increase in experiential learning. Many organizations are now implementing a model of development that strives for:

- 70% learning while on the job
- 20% learning from peers and colleagues
- 10% learning from classroom-style, traditional training.[2]

On the other hand, there are still many opportunities for learning and development to play a much bigger role in enhancing an organization's ability to optimize its talent. Significant room for gain surfaces in the areas of:

- Learning and development alignment to the leadership competencies and development gaps within the organization
- Coaching and mentoring skills of leaders within the organization
- Measuring the business impact of learning and development activities and initiatives.

We are reminded of an engagement we had with a multinational corporation. We were asked to do an audit of talent-optimization activities. As part

---

2. Based on the 70/20/10 learning model developed by Morgan McCall, Robert W. Eichinger, and Michael M. Lombardo at the Center for Creative Leadership (see Lombardo & Eichinger, 2007).

of our due diligence, we sat down with the well-intentioned professional in charge of leadership development and asked some basic questions.

- "How did you determine which learning and development offerings to provide?"
- "How do you assess the impact of the training your organization provides?"
- "How do you assure that the lessons and skills learned in training get utilized back on the job?"

Here is what we heard:

These are really, really great questions. Here at XYZ company, we like to offer all the typical stuff around how to be a manager, time management, and presentation skills. After every class, we provide the participants with a survey to gauge whether they felt they learned a lot from the curriculum. We closely look at these survey results to determine how to adjust the training materials and delivery. Now that last question . . . How do we assure that the training sticks, that the training is used back on the job? That to us is the $64,000 question. We give people great training, but often the learning they receive is not reinforced or role-modeled by their supervisors. Occasionally, I seek out individuals who attended a particular session, and I ask them how it is going and whether they are using the lessons we covered in class. All too often, I hear that they loved the session, but have not had a chance to practice what they learned. Worse, they may have a manager who laughed at what was covered in class. I wish I knew what we could do to get our leaders to be better role models and coaches. Once we get that, maybe we can figure out how our training initiatives support business success.

Learning and development efforts need to be much more strategic in nature and derived from both the business strategy and people strategy of the organization. Too often learning offerings are presented as "one-size-fits-all" solutions. To design and implement high-gain, talent-optimizing solutions, one must first be able to answer the following strategic alignment questions:

- Strategically, where has this organization been and what is the vision for where it is striving to go?
- Based on the business strategy, what are the most critical-to-success behaviors and skills needed by all leaders in the organization, not only for today, but also for tomorrow?
- Based on these "must-have" skills and competencies, what are our current talent gaps?

Once the answers to these strategic questions are understood, the opportunity exists to develop a learning and development strategy that is aligned with and supportive of increasing talent and business success. Then, the following five-pronged approach can be taken to instill learning and development as a significant advantage for the organization.

A Five-Pronged Approach to Learning and Development

Step 1: Assess correctly

All too often, a needs analysis is completed that becomes the anchor of the leadership development strategy, the leadership 360, and the basis for competencies required of leaders; however, it does not take into account whether the leaders really need these competencies or not.

A thorough assessment of leaders that uncovers gaps in competencies within the organization will enable a strategy to be developed that will address those specific gaps. A thorough assessment against future needs is also important. As a result, training initiatives are aimed at the gap areas, thus developing critical skills that are lacking.

Additionally, this level of focus grants a better opportunity to measure the impact of the training intervention. Training is customized to meet mass needs. With a good assessment, you can do both mass-focused training and individual development, which will result in improvement on the individual, team, and organization level.

Our research indicates that training and development is a strong lever to improve organization results and definitely should not be ignored. However, it needs to be more focused, more cost-effective, less classroom-driven, and measured more effectively for its impact to be realized.

Step 2: Keep focused on development that matters

The recent economic downturn has caused a massive reengineering in how training is delivered in organizations, if it is delivered at all. In some cases, this is a good thing, as older approaches needed to be rethought to be more innovative. However, our study indicated that, even in tough times, the top-tier companies did not let go of their leadership development initiatives. In fact, Susan Peters, General Electric's CLO, told *BusinessWeek* that development is not something GE will let leaders dismiss. She said it is critical to the organization's future success, but how training is delivered requires a rethink (Brady, 2010).

The old model of company training initiatives was a laundry list of classroom-driven courses linked to every aspect of its leadership model. Bringing leaders together in experiential settings requires a focus on the business strategy and what leaders need to learn to drive that strategy forward faster. Leaders learn to coach each other and work as a team to advance the business strategy. Learning groups are created in the classroom. These groups are sustained when the leaders return to the workplace and are prepared to tackle issues that confront the organization.

Step 3: Leverage social media

Social networking continues the learning after the classroom and creates space where people can dialogue in real time about what is working and what isn't. We are not saying that face-to-face training will go away. It won't and it shouldn't, but social networking will bleed more into the everyday fabric of the job. Of course, time has to be allocated for on-the-job reflection and dialogue and time is a very scarce commodity these days. But if you want people to grow and learn, you need to allocate time for it.

Step 4: Leverage coaching and peer mentoring

The next area for significant opportunity gain surfaces around coaching skills. Whether it is managers coaching their direct reports, peers coaching each other, or an individual serving to some extent as his or her own coach, the data tell us that coaching skills today are downright deplorable. This must change if an organization is to attain a talent advantage via talent sustainability. In our work with clients, we are just as likely to encounter managers who rely on the talent-destroyer techniques discussed earlier in this chapter as those who use the talent-optimizing behaviors that we will look at now. The best leaders in this area have the following characteristics:

- They care about their people.
- They are willing to give their time to others.
- They are excellent listeners.
- They place the needs of the organization ahead of their own needs.
- They set high standards for development and improvement.
- They establish specific goals and plans with each person they are coaching.
- They routinely provide candid, unvarnished feedback regarding behaviors and performance.

The strongest coaching organizations create a culture that is supportive of and values coaching efforts. It becomes a "must-have" characteristic and a prerequisite for advancement within the leadership ranks. These organizations ensure that managers receive training on behavioral coaching techniques (and can give Feed*Forward*) and that people development is a metric by which a manager's performance is measured.

Step 5: Measure progress and results

This leads to the final gap that the Talent Optimization Survey™ (TOS) found. Learning and development struggles mightily to assess the impact of talent development efforts. Whether it is measuring behavior or skill improvement in an individual or assessing the overall impact of development efforts on business metrics, most organizations have few, if any, concrete answers.

Most training departments measure training at the satisfaction level by asking participants what they gained from the training program. Some follow up three months later to see if the training has continued to be of use. Most of this evaluation, however, is self-evaluation, and as a consequence, suspect.

To test this theory that self-evaluation is suspect, we tried an exercise we heard about from Marshall Goldsmith (2007a). We asked a room full of leaders to close their eyes and raise their hand if they were a top performer. Nearly everyone raised their hand. No one said they were underperforming. The message here is that we generally have a much higher opinion of our capabilities than anyone else. It does not mean that people in this room were not top performers, but rather that they often couldn't see their gaps and what they needed to do to become more successful. The point is made that self-professed evaluations carry limited weight. Some companies do pre- and post-tests before and after a training program. However, these tests don't necessarily indicate whether the learning was lasting.

The most effective way to measure the impact of a development initiative is to be clear on your baseline. You get this baseline from doing an assessment, whether it is of an individual, a team, or an organization. The baseline must be established through some multirater approach. You then isolate the critical factors that need to be developed. You design the intervention and implement it. Then, you measure improvement, in 6-, 12- or 18-month intervals (depending on needs) around the critical factors, using the same raters that you used to establish the baseline.

Again, Marshall Goldsmith, a leading executive coach, builds this type of measurement into his coaching practice. He continues the measurement until the new skill becomes ingrained in the leader's DNA. While this may sound easy on the surface, it requires discipline and upfront planning in order to measure results. Busy leadership development professionals don't always have the time to do this. However, those who do will have job security for life. Your department will never become irrelevant and you will be sought after as a key advisor to drive change.

Pulling It All Together

So, what have we learned through our research? We have determined that learning and development does matter; however, the focus, methods, measures, and impacts must be strategically thought through in order for learning and development to make any appreciable difference. Think of yourself as developing a Net Promoter Score[3] for all of your learning initiatives whether you are a leader coaching others, a manager developing your team, or an HR professional charged with developing a learning culture. Remember:

- Classroom training has minimal impact, unless it is strategy driven and has an on-the-job component.
- Well-done assessment is the key to measuring success. Beware the needs-analysis trap.
- Coaching and feedback have proven to be some of the most powerful development tools—use them well. Build them into your culture, so that it is second nature for peers to ask for feedback and coaching that are helpful.
- Ensure that your leaders are able to do effective assessments of talent. Yes, we are harping on this throughout this book. You cannot give constructive feedback unless you can effectively assess behavior.
- Leverage career planning and have honest career discussions with people.
- Use assignments to develop skills. Build a learning plan into the assignment and measure learning throughout the assignment. Be explicit about what the assignment is meant to develop.
- Think ahead about next roles for your teams. Have a bigger picture for your people and work towards that picture.
- Give people space to have learning dialogues and build them into your business routines.
- Measure, measure, and measure again to show business relevance.
- Sharpen your own saw on creative ways to develop yourself and those who work with you.

---

3. Net Promoter is a management tool that can be used to gauge the loyalty of a firm's customer relationships. It serves as an alternative to traditional customer satisfaction research. (Wikipedia, accessed 08/27/10)

If you do the above, you will go a long way to creating a culture where learning is an everyday occurrence. People will want to go to development events because they know that these will enhance their career and give them a relevant business perspective or tool.

References

Brady, D. (2010, April 15). Can GE Still Manage? *Bloomberg Businessweek.* Retrieved September 9, 2010, from http://www.businessweek.com/magazine/content/10_17/b4175026765571.htm

Collins, J. (2009). *How the mighty fall: And why some companies never give in.* Self-published.

Goldsmith, M. (2002, 25, Summer). Try feed*forward* instead of feedback. *Leader to Leader.* Retrieved September 9, 2010, from http://www.marshallgoldsmithlibrary.com/cim/articles_display.php?aid=110

Goldsmith, M. (2007a, January/February). The success delusion: Why it can be so hard for successful leaders to change. *The Conference Board Review.* Retrieved September 9, 2010 from http://www.marshallgoldsmithlibrary.com/cim/articles_print.php?aid=667

CHAPTER 9

HUMAN RESOURCES CAPABILITY
The Keeper of Culture

Human resources (HR) has certainly evolved since the days we started in the field. However, it has not reached the heights that other functional areas, such as finance, marketing, risk management, and information systems, have. These functions are strategically linked to the core of the business. They have metrics that can be directly correlated to the bottom line.

HR, though, is still considered a "soft" discipline that handles problems with employees, benefits issues, time off, headcount, and layoffs. Many companies continue to view HR from an administrative rather than a strategic perspective. HR often lacks the rigor and discipline of the business, limitedly using tangible metrics and correlations tied to business results. Great leaders know how important HR is and that it is changing based on the approaches of successful companies. If you are not convinced, think how it is being dis-intermediated by technology.

With the advent of "self-service HR," automating or outsourcing administrative duties such as handling headcount, benefits, pensions, etc., more of the other responsibilities, especially strategic ones, are being placed on the shoulders of managers and leaders. As HR moves away from administrative work, it will be forced to play more of a strategic role to be a value-add to companies. This shift toward automating HR will have a most profound effect, as systems and groups can handle the administrative duties much faster, more effectively, and cheaper than an internal HR department. So what will HR professionals do to keep themselves relevant in the next ten years? We contend that they will become:

1. Chief culture officers
2. Top-notch executive coaches
3. Outstanding talent assessors
4. Expert organizational strategists
5. Masters in talent analytics.

Chief Culture Officers

In chapter 4, we discussed the power of culture and its relationship to having the best talent. However, we did not address who is responsible for ensuring that the organization maintains the culture that it requires for success. We would argue that this is a critical role of HR professionals. Since their jobs are about people and how they relate to the performance of the organization, it is only natural that HR leaders should be the "keepers of the culture." While we have established that leaders should create the culture, HR professionals should ensure that leaders are in fact living the values that they espouse. To do this, HR professionals need to understand culture, have frameworks to assess it, and be able to demonstrate the link between culture and bottom line.

The last decade has seen an erosion of values in organizations. From the scandals of Enron, Tyco, and Worldcom in the early 2000s to the greed that has become apparent in Wall Street during the recent economic meltdown, organizations have taken their eyes off the ethical ball. This is not because people are inherently bad and want to cheat others, but because few people during these times were doing more than paying lip service to corporate values. No one was making sure that the organizations' leaders were embodying corporate values in the face of tough pressures to perform and show a strong bottom line.

Most publicly traded companies now have codes of conduct or statements around integrity. However, few do more than train their staff in the codes of conduct. As long as the "box is checked" that employees have taken an (in most cases) online training course, that's enough. This has limited effect on redirecting business cultures toward integrity over the bottom line.

In a recent article, Hope Greenfield, former chief talent officer of Lehman Brothers, claimed that, in large part, that organization's culture was ultimately a factor in its demise (Greenfield, 2009). No one was ensuring that the culture evolved in a positive way that supported the growth of the company. First and foremost, companies need to have values that they live by and a lens to ensure that their leaders are living by these values. Who better to ensure that values are in place and behaviors aligned in leaders than HR professionals?

At Benedictine University's Center for Values-Driven Leadership, we have worked closely with the research team led by Director James Ludema. By identifying the conditions that support a strong values-based culture, we have built a values-integration model that allows HR professionals to identify the actions they can take to efficiently and effectively integrate organizational values into all levels of the organization. (See chapter 9 appendix.) The values-integration model can help HR professionals to better diagnose an action plan for how to build a supportive, values-based culture. In addition, there are many other data sources that are excellent indicators of whether leaders are living the values of the organization:

- Cultural assessment: we have discussed numerous ways to quantify your culture in this book;
- Exit interviews: determine the "real why" employees are leaving;
- Employee satisfaction and engagement surveys: not only the scores, but also the comments, which are much more informative;

- Customer interviews and surveys to gauge how external stakeholders view the organization's culture and values;
- Ombudsman complaints and employee grievances.

All of these tools help spotlight the key behaviors, values, and cultural norms that are at play within an organization.

Top-Notch Executive Coaches

In our talent optimization work, we have found that coaching is a critical factor that correlates talent with business results. This should be music to the ears of HR professionals, who often have to fight tooth and nail to get support and funding for development initiatives. Beyond creating the development framework for the organization, HR professionals are in a great position to leverage their unique understanding of how leadership behaviors and organizational culture link to business results and high performance. They are well positioned to be internal executive coaches to their business leaders. To ensure that the business and talent strategy are fully supporting each other, HR professionals need to coach leaders in how to align their behaviors in accord with what is needed to create a high-performance culture.

To lead organizations on a successful talent-optimization journey, HR professionals will not only need to coach leaders, they will also need to teach these same leaders how to coach their teams. Through our work in assessing the behaviors of leaders in the past five years, we have unearthed a disturbing trend: fewer and fewer leaders and managers are investing time in the coaching of their team members. Our interviews with leaders display a great deal of intent around coaching, and even an enjoyment of coaching direct reports. However, we have found too little "real" action in this area. Helping leaders to create a simple, repeatable routine for having positive, future-focused, career conversations with employees is a must-do for HR professionals, as these discussions can increase employee engagement and reduce unwanted turnover. Most leaders do want to coach their employees, but few have an effective and efficient model to do so. Providing and teaching a model that leaders can use to create a culture of coaching, constructive feedback, and future-focused support presents a prime opportunity for HR professionals. To meet this exciting challenge, HR professionals must first and foremost be effective coaches themselves, have one or more proven and effective models to use, and have the credibility within the organization to play this role.

Barriers to HR Coaching Credibility

There are several factors that erode the credibility of HR people in playing this role:

1. Lack of confidentiality: not being trusted to hold discussions in confidence and using outcomes of discussions in other arenas that effect an employee's career;
2. Inability to provide insight because of a lack of ability to effectively assess talent;
3. Inability to help others see or uncover their aspirations and the skills necessary to achieve them;
4. Not being a role model for the values of the organization;
5. Not being open to feedback and/or honest about their own strengths and development needs;
6. Limited time available due to workload on tactical/reactive issues;
7. Not viewed as a strategic partner by business leaders.

See chapter 9 appendix for our coaching assessment checklist. Please take a look to see how you are doing in this area.

In order to counteract these potential pitfalls to HR professionals being effective executive coaches, we suggest the following actions:

- Ensure that they participate in business leader meetings and are grounded in the business strategies of the organization.
- Require them to be trained in coaching as a core competency for the HR development model.
- Certify that internal coaches are at the level of proficiency of any top-notch external executive coach.
- Allow coachees to select their coach from several options. Chemistry is a big part of coaching. Do not have anyone coach someone formally who is from the same division or group.
- Ensure that the coach uses a coaching contract and that clear measures for success are identified and tracked.
- Measure and track the effectiveness of the coaching. We like to use brief behavior surveys that track the progress. (See sample in chapter 9 appendix. We also advocate including questions about the organization's coaching capacity in employee surveys).
- Continually monitor the quality of your coaches. If someone does not meet the requirements above, take action.

There will always be a place for external coaches and rightly so, but not everyone in the organization can have an external coach. We suggest that you pick your external coaches wisely. Use them to help good leaders get better. Do not use them for remedial purposes or as the last step before letting someone go: Using coaches in this way will do exactly the opposite of developing a coaching culture and will cause executives to avoid coaching altogether.

We subscribe to the model created by Marshall Goldsmith and Howard Morgan (2000) in "Team Building without Time Wasting" as a means of helping to build skills and change behavior. It is a fun approach that any skilled HR professional can master and utilize to support team building within a work unit. It is simple and opens team members up to helping each other become better instead of competing against each other. Goldsmith and Morgan guide you through how this process works and explain the power it can provide. We have personally used it with great success. This approach helps team members understand that others on the team often have the same issues and that it can be fun to get ideas for improvement from them. Finally, it can help build trust and rapport.

Outstanding Talent Assessors

In our opinion, HR professionals need to be the role models for accurate and insightful talent assessment. While everyone in an organization makes assessments about the people around them on a daily basis, most people fall prey to their own unique biases when assessing others. This is where HR professionals need to demonstrate expertise and leadership.

HR professionals are the best positioned and trained to provide frameworks and methodologies for conducting accurate and reliable assessments. However, to date, there has not been a strong enough push to create assessment guidelines for ensuring that proven methods rooted in science are fully leveraged by leaders within organizations. Therefore, managers are often left to their own instincts and skills to conduct assessments of job candidates and incumbent talent. How can this be a prudent practice? It is not. It is a practice that can short circuit talent optimization. Would a successful company leave the assessment of financial performance versus metrics to the instincts or best guesses of managers?

To demonstrate leadership and expertise in the area of talent assessment, HR professionals must first become outstanding talent assessors themselves. This requires a deep understanding of the skills, behaviors, and motivations that support successful performance in defined job roles. Additionally, HR professionals should have a complete toolbox of options for effectively assessing talent, and they should seek opportunities to refine and improve their own assessment skills and expertise. Within the assessment toolbox, there should be a number of tested and reliable assessment practices, including:

- Behavioral interviewing
- Biographical interviewing—the resume walk
- Paired interviewing
- Work simulations and role-playing
- Behavioral observation
- Multirater 360 feedback tools
- Validated personality and cognitive skills assessments.

HR professionals need to be able to effectively conduct assessments using the above techniques and they should be effective teachers and coaches to others in the organization. By building the skill sets of the leaders who are in a position to assess and evaluate behaviors and performance on a daily basis, HR professionals assist in the creation of a significant competitive advantage for their organizations.

Finally, HR professionals need to demonstrate leadership in the creation of a clear assessment strategy for the organization as a whole, and ensure that HR team members are well trained in the models and tools that are used. Additionally, HR professionals need to proactively track the quality of decisions made in the selection, promotion/demotion, and succession planning processes. For any talent movement made, there should be an effort to collect data regarding the quality of the decision.

A high-tech Fortune 50 client that we have does an excellent job of evaluating the quality of assessment decisions. For each person that exits the organization and is replaced by a new hire, there is a process in place to gauge whether the new hire is indeed an improvement over the individual who has departed. This allows the organization to carefully track overall talent improvement in the organization over time.

Expert Organizational Strategists

This role is significantly different from that of the business strategist. The purpose of this position is to make the necessary organizational adjustments in terms of people, process, and structure to align the organization to business needs. This is easier said than done.

Deep knowledge of organizational development will be required for this to be successful. In particular, expert organizational strategists will need to:

- Drive change and understand effective change methodologies, e.g., Appreciative Inquiry, Change Acceleration Process (CAP), and Future Search;
- Align communications to the change process;
- Understand the psychology of bringing people along with the organization's journey;
- Structure organizations for the most effective delivery against the strategy;
- Know the most important skill gaps and how to go about closing them beyond training—how and where to recruit for talent and how to develop pipelines;
- Understand how to quickly and effectively ramp up a team's performance through structured team-building approaches;
- Assess the current state of affairs from an organizational point of view that enables staff members to work more effectively together;
- Move quickly to integrate the people aspects of an integration or acquisition—effectively get people on board and feeling part of the new organization;
- Understand how to diagnose an organization and design effective methods to close gaps.

These are just some of the examples of what HR professionals will be required to do to add value. We see pockets of brilliance in these areas, but organizational strategizing is still a much underused skill set. Additionally, we see people who have learned organizational development techniques and who are good facilitators, but who lack the depth of knowledge and learning in this area to be truly effective. We see more "operational" HR people who can drive layoffs, do compensation plans, and run staffing on a day-to-day basis; they can keep people out of trouble from an employee-relations point of view.

However, few HR people possess the organizational development skills required to drive organizational alignment and to provide critical data-driven insights to leaders. Leaders need this type of assistance so they can keep themselves, their teams, and the organization consistently on the path of high performance. There is nothing worse than relying on an organizational development facilitator who does not have depth of knowledge about how organizations work, how teams develop, how to grow leaders, and how to drive change. To combat this dilemma, we recommend formal training in organizational development for HR professionals. It should be a core competency for anyone wishing to partner in making the business perform to its fullest potential.

Masters in Talent Analytics

Talent analytics—evaluating program impact and the degree of change it provides— requires a thorough understanding of measurement and metrics. Experts in this area are becoming increasingly important to organizations. In particular, it is important to know how to:

- Collect data and diagnose information that will inform the system
- Create questionnaires and interview protocols
- Quantify and communicate observations in terms that resonate with business leaders

We have seen many homespun surveys used with much data collected; however, all too often, the data do little to inform the organization on which processes and systems are highly effective and which ones need significant changes in order to support business success. Talent analytics is emerging as a science, and HR professionals need to work hand in hand with talent researchers to collect, interpret, and explain the data in a manner that educates senior executives and supports talent optimization.

Talent analytics masters know what qualitative tools are available and which quantitative tools will accurately measure the intervention being used. They understand the best techniques for collecting and analyzing data, and have a base command of statistics. It's no small feat to demonstrate the links and correlations between talent actions and business results, but it must be done!

The HR talent analytics masters of the future will be looked upon for expertise and insights similar to the way we look at an organization's market research department today. Market researchers measure customers' preferences and buying patterns using sophisticated data-gathering and statistical models. With these tools, a good marketing department can inform and educate the organization on the actions that should be taken to increase market share and draw in new customers. Moving forward, this same precision should be expected from HR talent analytics masters to guide organizational interventions and talent outcomes.

By rigorously asking the right questions, using a solid research design, and applying the right analytics, it is possible to determine:

- Who will be successful in the organization and who will not,
- The four or five skills that are most critical for business results,

- The correlation of leadership behaviors to high-performance outcomes and marketplace results,
- When talent actions are falling out of alignment with business needs.

Without experts in talent analytics, it is likely that organizations will continue to be ill-informed about what they are doing well and what they need to do differently. The following case study exemplifies this point.

A company instituted a new mentoring program because its leaders believed that mentoring was the key to driving diversity. The organization trained employees, assigned mentors to them, and had them complete surveys to evaluate the effectiveness of the program. However, when the survey questions were analyzed, they were the same old questions we so often see coming out of HR departments:

- How did you connect with your mentor?
- Do you feel better about your career because you have a mentor?
- How effective was your training?
- How effective was your mentor?

These questions might sound okay, but nothing in them is tied to meaningful results. They do not address the "so what" factor, or why the program was created in the first place: to drive increased retention and promote diverse talent. Questions aligned to retention would have been more telling, e.g., "What is your intent to stay with the organization?" The answers could then have been correlated with retention and promotion data. The main point here is that it is essential to know what questions to ask, what data will answer the questions, what methods to use to collect the data, and how to analyze the data.

If you are an HR professional looking to get a seat at the table, ponder the characteristics cited above. Can you extend your focus from the quality of your HR services to the impact that those services are having on the organization? What would your company say about you and your skill set? What would your customers say about you and your skills? Develop a personal action plan to build your brand as an HR strategist and talent analytics guru.

If you are a leader looking for a top-notch HR professional to support you, ask yourself the following questions:

- Can this person analyze business problems effectively, apply analytics, and design practical solutions?

- Is this person effective at developing leaders and can he or she be a credible and effective coach?
- Can this person candidly and accurately assess talent?
- Can this person create strategic organization and workforce plans that make a difference and how does he or she show the impact from those plans?
- Does this person understand the business and how it makes money?
- Does this person speak the language of the business?
- Does this person have a deep understanding and true practice in driving change and in strategic organizational development?

References

Goldsmith, M. & Morgan, H. (2000) Team building without time wasting. In M. Goldsmith, L. Lyons, & Alyssa Freas. (Eds). *Coaching for leadership: how the world's greatest coaches help leaders learn* (pp. 103–109).

Greenfield, H. (2009, Fall). Culture clash. *The Conference Board Review.* Retrieved September 9, 2010, from http://www.tcbreview.com/culture-crash.php

APPENDIX 9:
ORGANIZATIONAL VALUES INVENTORY (OVI):
CREATING A VALUES-DRIVEN ORGANIZATION
TO SUPPORT BUSINESS PERFORMANCE

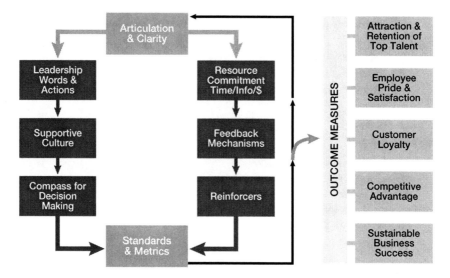

OVI: TYPES OF ORGANIZATIONS

HIGH

"Poor Investment"

Minimal bang for the buck; high investment, lower than expected outcomes due to low leadership engagement and cultural support

"Values as a Competitive Advantage"

Values-driven company – alignment of leadership behaviors, culture, processes, systems, and reinforcers drives high performance and sustainable business results

"Destructive Values"

Breeding ground for a toxic culture, unethical behavior, a loss of trust with stakeholders, and poor performance

"Poor Alignment"

Leader-organization disconnect; values less pronounced as they cascade down the organization; disconnected from business performance

VALUES PROCESSES AND SYSTEMS

LOW

LOW   VALUES LEADERSHIP AND CULTURE   HIGH

RATE YOURSELF ON THE PERSONAL ATTRIBUTES OF A GOOD EXECUTIVE COACH

Always (5)   Frequently (4)   50/50 (3)   Rarely (2)   Never (1)

	Always (5)	Frequently (4)	50/50 (3)	Rarely (2)	Never (1)
1. **Positive** – focus on productivity goals to achieve peak performance	5	4	3	2	1
2. **Future focused** – looks ahead, not dwelling on or correcting past mistakes	5	4	3	2	1
3. **Unbiased** – does not get influenced by past experiences; is not judgmental	5	4	3	2	1
4. **Enthusiastic** – looks for ways to achieve success, not why things won't work	5	4	3	2	1
5. **Supportive** – anticipates needs and prevents problems	5	4	3	2	1
6. **Trusting** – believes people are trying to do their best	5	4	3	2	1
7. **Is specific** – narrows things to manageable tasks; helps people focus on a clear goal	5	4	3	2	1
8. **Knowledgeable** – knows what you are talking about	5	4	3	2	1
9. **Observant** – is aware of what isn't said as well as what is; keeps eyes and ears open	5	4	3	2	1
10.**Respectful** – acknowledges differences and shows sensitivity to the individual	5	4	3	2	1
11.**Assertive** – asserts with confidence and persistence	5	4	3	2	1
12.**Confidential** – maintains confidence and does not share discussions with others	5	4	3	2	1
13.**Listens** – pays attention to what's being said; maintains eye contact	5	4	3	2	1
14.**Seeks to clarify** – asks questions to seek understanding	5	4	3	2	1

CHAPTER 10

TALENT DATA ANALYTICS
High-Impact Measurement that Matters

Optimizing Talent, pages 125–137
Copyright © 2011 by Information Age Publishing

When a leader at any level of an organization wants to make an investment of company time, resources, and money, she goes to great lengths to build a data-based rationale for why the investment makes "good business sense." Relevant data are gathered and organized into an elaborate series of spreadsheets and charts in an effort to build an impenetrable case in support of the benefits of the investment. At the proper time, a flawless presentation is delivered to the leaders in control of resources, the purpose of which is to demonstrate the business rationale and to illustrate the expected return from the investment. Quite often these presentations are filled with concrete facts and figures that lend credibility and credence to the investment under consideration.

Most corporations in which we have worked have an abundance of highly intelligent, right-brained MBAs who are blessed with the skill set of data analytics. These data crunchers can take anything tangible, countable, and stackable and quickly identify how a reduction in one area can lead to a measurable gain in another area. Many of the quality-based, Six Sigma projects we have witnessed follow this logical path. Leaders identify a business issue or problem, survey what stackable data can be collected, and devise well-thought-out interventions, which are typically aimed at increased business efficiencies, process improvements, and cost reductions. This data-based approach to solving business problems has become the "price of admission" needed to gain the support and sponsorship of top-level executives. These executives require a straightforward, clearly articulated set of analytics if they are to support and sponsor a proposed course of action.

Unfortunately, the world of talent optimization has not yet evolved to the level required when it comes to data analytics. The issues and obstacles are obvious. Up until now,

- Talent leaders and managers have only been scratching the surface of understanding what conditions lead to human performance.
- Business schools have not emphasized the important skills and processes for assessing, developing, and engaging talent.
- There has been very little focus on gathering the data needed to demonstrate the connections between talent actions and business outcomes.

Because of these factors, many leaders are left to trust their own formulas and recipes for securing and optimizing talent on their teams and in their organizations. This creates a climate in which leaders fall prey to the latest leadership development fads and gimmicks. With no clear data analyses that demonstrate how actions and outcomes are linked, it is nearly impossible to get senior leader support for creating and implementing a systemic, integrated approach to talent optimization. Until the field of talent optimization has the data-based sophistication of finance, quality management, market research, and engineering, organizations will continue to make serious errors in the areas of talent acquisition, development, and engagement.

To illustrate these points, let's revisit our bright-eyed talent manager from chapter 2. Recall that this leader stepped into a situation in which all components of the Talent Optimization Framework™ (TOF) were "broken." Try to picture yourself being in his shoes, or the shoes of any leader who has come into an organization in which talent management is dysfunctional. Picture a negative culture in which talent is underappreciated and team members are discouraged, an environment that has no talent strategy and in which hiring decisions are made based on intuition versus rigor. Imagine leading in a company with little in the way of meaningful training, where the performance appraisal is treated like a check-the-box, bureaucratic process. We suspect that many of you are getting the sinking feeling that we are writing about one of your previous employers. Without a clear understanding of the TOF and without the data needed to demonstrate the causal relationships between taking the appropriate talent actions and attaining positive results, talent managers and leaders at all levels of the organization are at a loss to fix talent gaps or to get the support from their sponsors to invest in the right talent solutions.

Contrast this situation with one in which a new service manager enters an organization and within the first week on the job is presented with "black and white" data regarding the service effectiveness of the organization (see Table 10.1).

While the new service manager has an unenviable set of challenges ahead of her, she is well positioned with "hard" data and metrics to help guide her plans and track progress. Most importantly, she has the business

TABLE 10.1 Organizational Effectiveness Chart

	Your Company	Industry Benchmarks
Customer Complaints/Month	45	30
Service Response Time	7 Days	3 Days
Average Cost of Service Call	$2,000	$1,500
Customer Satisfaction	65%	85%

metrics necessary to gain the attention, support, and buy-in of her senior leaders and sponsors.

When it comes to talent optimization, the undeniable truths are:

1. People are the most important ingredient to almost every organization's success.
2. The science of talent optimization lags far behind many other business disciplines in the areas of collecting the right data, analytics of the data, and linking the talent data to important metrics of business performance.
3. To secure the support and resource commitments from senior leaders, talent optimization metrics linked to meaningful organizational outcome measures must be established.
4. With people oftentimes being the largest budget item within organizations, leaders and talent managers who crack the code on talent data analytics will create unparalleled competitive advantage, employee productivity, sustainability, and shareholder value for their organizations.

The TOF is meant to provide the integrated model, data road map, and metrics required so that leaders at all levels can play a critical role in creating value for their teams and organizations. With these tools in hand, leaders will have a clear path to follow for collecting talent data, linking talent efforts to business outcomes, and building the business case for talent optimization efforts.

As scholars and practitioners who have more than 40 years of combined experience in the field of talent optimization, we are certain that a game-changing talent revolution is an absolute necessity if companies are to ensure sustainability and growth. This field needs to leverage the brilliant MBAs and Six Sigma black belts to unleash their analytical talents in order to help organizations:

- Collect the relevant data around each TOF lever
- Objectively diagnose the current state of talent
- Shape plans for closing talent optimization gaps
- Assess and document progress along the way
- Link TOF data to specific business outcomes
- Build a data-rich case for senior executives on the absolute importance of the TOF

Talent Optimization: Gathering, Interpreting, and Leveraging the Right Talent Data

In developing the Talent Optimization Framework and Survey™, we wanted to provide clarity for leaders and practitioners regarding the areas upon which to focus when collecting talent data. The challenge is to have a clear line of sight to the rich data points that make a difference, and not to get caught in the data analysis–paralysis trap. To illustrate this point, we asked survey respondents questions regarding how their organizations collect, store, and analyze their talent data. What we learned is the following:

- Companies are spending lots of time and money in getting data collection and storage systems up and running, while
- Little time is spent analyzing the data for decision making and assessing business impacts!

Our initial emphasis on data storage within the survey items led to our finding that data storage by itself is not a strong lever for driving positive talent outcomes. By separating the survey items that focus on data analytics from the data storage items, we found that companies that collect and effectively analyze their talent data are much more likely to experience better business outcomes. Thus, we have adjusted our thinking and now believe that the true power of storage systems is not in having them, but rather in having access to the right data and using that data to create analytic-based insights. Put simply, systems are only as good as the data in them, and being strategic and clear about which data to collect and how to analyze this data gets to the core of the issue. In the following pages, we will provide you with the specific areas in which you will need to gather data and show you how to use that data for effective decision making.

To make a compelling case for the development of effective talent practices, you will first need to quantify the data that you obtain. We find that a good practice in this area is to utilize a 7-point scale in rating the organization's effectiveness in each portion of the TOF. Think of the TOF as a GPS that points you in the direction of the data that are most important to collect and understand. We refer to this as the *macro data collection level*. This level tells you where you need to focus in order to get to your final destination. The TOF enables you to have this big picture or whole-systems view of your talent strategy and points you to the most important areas that you need to address to get the most improvement. In addition to the systemic, macro view, there is also a micro level of data you will need as well. This micro level consists of the data you need to collect in order to track, measure, and assess the effectiveness of your talent strategy execution. It is when you have the macro, strategic view, and the micro, tactical view working in concert that you are on the path to leveraging data analytics as a key component to talent optimization for your organization.

As we learned in our survey of business leaders, there is no shortage of HR data collected throughout most organizations. The questions become, "Is this the right data?" and "Does this data truly inform decision making?" All too often, the answer to both questions is a resounding "No!" While there may be many reasons for this, we see three central causes:

1. Not formulating the right questions
2. Not collecting the correct data
3. Not conducting rigorous data analysis

A historical corollary to this can be found in the early days of companies implementing Six Sigma to drive quality improvements. These companies and their employees often lacked an understanding of the basic data necessary to answer their compelling business questions. This hampered their ability to make informed decisions about how to improve and assess the current state of affairs, let alone develop effective process changes for the future. This appears to be where talent analytics are today. The field of talent data analytics is just now emerging from a focus on data gathering and storage, and is still in its infancy when it comes to analysis driving break-through talent solutions and business outcomes. What follows is a list of provocative and targeted questions we often hear from CEOs and senior leaders. These questions require the right data to be collected and analyzed in order to move toward talent optimization:

- Do we have an effective talent strategy?
- Do we have the best talent in our most important roles?
- Are we rewarding our top performers appropriately?
- Are we retaining our best people?
- Why are some groups or teams more engaged than others?
- Why is the performance of one team higher/lower than others?
- Do we have innovative thinking going on in our organization?
- Do we have a sufficient pipeline of great talent to quickly move into larger roles?
- Are we hiring the best talent in the market?
- Do our people have the capability to compete in tomorrow's game?
- Do we have the right people in the right jobs?

- Are we constantly raising the bar and improving the capability of our talent?
- How do we increase the capability of a group to outperform its competitors?
- Is this improved talent capability improving our market performance?

While this is not meant to be an exhaustive list of talent-related questions, it does represent the themes we have heard over and over again from senior business and HR leaders. These leaders want assurances that their organizations "have the best talent" and are "doing the right things to develop the talent necessary to compete in the marketplace of the future." These are very difficult goals to achieve without the ability to collect the right data and conduct the proper statistical analysis.

Data that Matter

In order to answer the questions above, we recommend that, at a minimum, you collect data in five areas. First, we'll start with the TOF.

As a refresher, the TOF has eight critical levers:

1. Leadership Engagement
2. Supportive Culture
3. Strategic Alignment
4. Talent Assessment
5. Performance Management
6. Learning and Development
7. Human Resources Capability
8. Data and Storage Analytics

Using this survey will tell you the specific levers of the TOF that are currently assets for your organization and which are problem areas. With the TOF results, you can clearly understand what contributes most to business outcomes and what is dragging a particular group down. You can go a step further and determine the specific items within a lever that need to be addressed to drive improvement. This assessment gives you a clear reading of the overall health of your talent strategy and points you to solutions by proffering hard proof of what is working and what needs to be fixed. It is your call to action. We have provided a link in the final chapter of the book that allows you to use the Talent Optimization Survey™ (TOS) to begin to get a baseline measure of where your organization is on each lever.

To take your analysis to the next level and understand the correlations that are linked to performance and results, we recommend that you collect data from the following four sources:

1. Leadership Assessment Data: You need to assess your leaders against a set of criteria/competencies that we discussed at great length in chapter 6.
2. Cultural Assessment Data: You need to diagnose what type of culture you have and how it supports or takes away from talent optimization.
3. Employee Engagement and Satisfaction Data: You need to understand how engaged and satisfied your employees and team members are.
4. Customer Satisfaction Data: This needs to include both external customer feedback on company performance and internal customer feedback on various departments and functions.

With this information in hand, you can start analyzing the data, developing insights, and answering many of the above questions. What follows are some simple examples of how this can be done.

With some organizations, we leverage the TOS to identify the best-performing and lowest-performing regions and functions. We cross check this data with business outcome data that display how each group is performing versus goals. Next, we help organizations isolate the unique skills sets and practices of the top-performing groups versus the lower-performing groups. We call this a "Gap Analysis" study. We often use statistical tests to assess the significance of these differences. Once we are sure of the gaps, we are ready to posit potential solutions for closing them. Here is an interesting and realistic question for you to consider: Are your leaders and managers who are best at meeting day-to-day numbers the same leaders who are best at optimizing talent? Collect and analyze data from the TOF and the four key categories listed above. Correlate scores on business outcomes with scores gathered on talent optimization, and see what you find.

Here is another straightforward scenario that leverages data analytics. If you want to know whether a learning intervention is improving a group's performance, compare the group receiving the learning to a like group that is not receiving the same developmental opportunity. Again, use a standard statistical test to identify whether the differences are indeed significant and whether the intervention is showing a reasonable ROI.

If your employee engagement scores are low in a particular area, take a deeper dive into the leadership skills and the cultural dimensions identified by the TOF. Statistically validate which skills and cultural elements are contributing most to the low engagement scores and develop interventions to close the gaps. Correlate the low engagement scores with the financial performance of the group and/or customer satisfaction data and track improvement in these areas as the unit improves. Statistics and asking the right questions turn data into powerful information that underscores the value and impact of talent optimization.

We highlighted another powerful story in chapter 9 about a company that quantifiably demonstrated that it was increasing the capability of certain business units by improving hiring practices. HR leaders had isolated the critical high-performance skills they were looking for, hired and promoted to those skills, and could compare the previous team to the new team to show significant results. The next step along this path would be to show increased market performance as a result of the improved leadership capability, as well as an increase in employee and customer satisfaction. To take this example one step further, find out what are the best teams' track records for retention. You get the picture. This is powerful information that will be crucial to collect and analyze in order to optimize talent and to provide the proof points that senior executives often want prior to making talent investments. We have provided a few examples for you to consider; we hope that we have sparked a fire within you to join the crusade for increased rigor and talent optimization analytics!

To further bring talent analytics to life, we would like to share a real-life case study from our talent consulting work. In this particular situation, we received a call from the new VP of a multinational corporation with over $10 billion in funds under management and approximately 10,000 employees. The company was considered a blue chip company in its market. The situation the VP faced is typical of what we have seen in many of our customer organizations. In this case, however, talent data analytics provided the information needed to gain senior leader support and to enact positive and measurable change in the organization.

A Case in Action

The VP of HR walked into an organization that had never thought about an integrated framework for talent optimization. The presenting issues were as follows:

- Senior leaders were concerned about the lack of up-and-coming leaders in the organization. "Why don't we have the leadership depth we need to grow our business?"

- ▪ The HR team was concerned about the ongoing and future exits of key performers due to low engagement and a lack of clear career paths. "Why are so many of our younger, up-and-coming professionals leaving us to join our competitors?"
- ▪ The employees were concerned about potential layoffs and had a sense that management was only focused on financial results and not people development. "Why do the leaders here seem consumed with cutting everything to the bone while investing so little in our development and growth?"

The Data Gathering

As the new kid on the block, the VP of HR took advantage of her perceived naiveté to conduct thorough due diligence. She utilized the Talent Optimization Framework and Survey™ to gather the perspectives of the leadership team, HR community, and line managers around the state of talent optimization in the organization. All told, 64 stakeholders completed the TOS.

The Key Results

The survey results clearly revealed that there were a number of talent optimization issues to improve upon, as well as a few definitive strengths (the lighter blocks in the figure below) to leverage in the organization. (See Figure 10.1.)

The VP now had reliable data showing that the key enablers of the framework (leadership and culture) scored sufficiently well. She now knew that the organization had a good foundation upon which to build a talent roadmap.

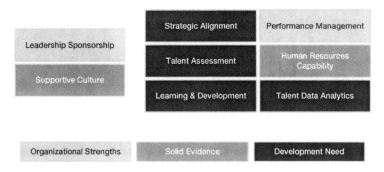

Figure 10.1 The Talent Optimization Framework™.

The data also lent support to the effectiveness of the current performance management processes. This helped to validate the recent work the HR leaders had done to update and improve the impact and effectiveness of performance reviews. From a glass-half-full standpoint, the new VP had much to feel good about.

Now she turned to the areas of deficit that came through from the talent survey. It became clear that little to no work had been done to align business and people strategies. The company was moving into new arenas to generate revenue (getting into custom solutions and consulting offerings), but there were no articulated plans for how to assess and develop people in order to ensure effective performance in these new arenas.

Let's take a look at the following line chart to illustrate the talent optimization gaps within this company. (See Figure 10.2.)

By utilizing the framework and gathering data from the right stakeholders, the talent optimization issues became much clearer. In addition, the external norms provided by the authors and linkage to measures of business results and outcomes got the full attention of the executive leadership team.

With the key talent levers understood and the organizational gaps identified, the HR leader was able to initiate a number of the assessment, development, and data analytics practices highlighted throughout this book. In

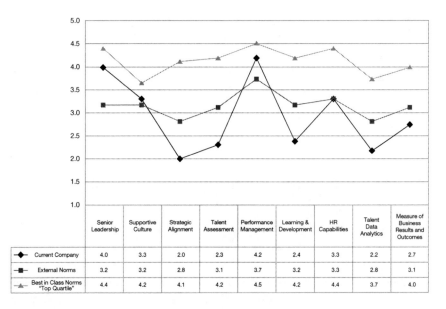

	Senior Leadership	Supportive Culture	Strategic Alignment	Talent Assessment	Performance Management	Learning & Development	HR Capabilities	Talent Data Analytics	Measure of Business Results and Outcomes
◆ Current Company	4.0	3.3	2.0	2.3	4.2	2.4	3.3	2.2	2.7
■ External Norms	3.2	3.2	2.8	3.1	3.7	3.2	3.3	2.8	3.1
▲ Best in Class Norms "Top Quartile"	4.4	4.2	4.1	4.2	4.5	4.2	4.4	3.7	4.0

Figure 10.2   Talent optimization normative comparison.

addition, she was able to develop clear metrics and scorecards for tracking progress within each talent arena. After just six months of focused effort, the talent optimization metrics displayed significant improvement. In addition, the HR team was able to go back to the three questions that had the organization in turmoil and provide factual, data-based responses:

1. "Why don't we have the leadership depth we need to grow our business?"
2. "Why are so many of our younger, up-and-coming professionals leaving us to join our competitors?"
3. "Why do the leaders here seem consumed with adding more work, cutting everything to the bone while investing so little in our development and growth?"

They could now see that the core issue that led to these questions centered on the lack of strategic alignment. While business strategies were well articulated and new services were being offered, emerging leaders were not being developed in the new competencies and skill sets needed to succeed. Young talented people were becoming disgruntled by their lack of growth or understanding of how they fit into the future of the company and thus became prime targets for search firms and competitor advances. Lastly, the rank-and-file saw that the company was changing, but felt left behind in their own development and growth.

In this instance, the TOF and assessment of the levers that are significantly correlated with talent optimization provided the HR leader with the tools and data to build a business case for strategic alignment, and improved assessment and development. In addition, the HR team demonstrated to the rest of the executive leadership team that HR was fully capable of analyzing data, tracking outcomes, and creating measurable business improvements to enhance the current and future sustainability of the organization.

How Do You Get Started Being a Talent Data Analyst?

Whether you know it or not, you probably already have the skills necessary to be a talent data analyst; it's just a matter of applying them to your talent optimization thought processes. You use them every day when you are thinking about customers or the financial performance of your business. As Thomas Davenport and Jeanne Harris point out in *Competing on Analytics* (2007), using data collection and analysis allows you to determine what customers want, how loyal they are to you and your products, and what they are willing to pay for your services. The same approach can be applied to your people by applying some of the same logic.

We recommend the following steps:

- Formulate questions that matter: What keeps you up at night about your talent?
- Do a bit of research on what data exist and what best practices are out there
- Determine the data needed to answer the questions
- Review the data and if you don't have what you need, start collecting it
- Conduct statistical analyses
- Leverage the data insights in talent decision making

You don't have to be a statistical expert, but you do need to know what questions to ask and you may need to find someone who can do this type of analysis for you. These people do exist somewhere in your organization. If you want to get a bit more familiar with data analytics, we recommend the following books: *Statistics: A Self-Teaching Guide* (Fourth edition, John Wiley & Sons, 1997) by Donald J. Koosis. This book will give you a general understanding of statistics, data collection, and analysis so you know what questions to ask and generally how to analyze data. *People Productivity: A Validated Model for Measurement* (Ponte Verdra Beach, FL: Work Systems Associates, 1989) by Harold S. Resnick and H. Sandy Brown. This book will help you think about how to measure productivity of people.

Following the steps described above is exactly how we went about creating the TOF. Through our research and data analytics, we set out to help others by taking the guesswork out of what really matters when it comes to optimizing talent and creating positive business results. The data we have collected and the analyses we have conducted have led us to be able to say with the utmost confidence that the TOF will yield truly powerful business outcomes.

References

Davenport, T. H., & Harris, J. G. (2007). *Competing on analytics: The new science of winning.* Boston: Harvard Business School Press.

Koosis, D. J. (1997). Statistics: A self-teaching guide (4th ed.). New York: John Wiley & Sons.

Resnick, H.S., & Brown, H. S. (1989). People productivity: A validated model for measurement. Ponte Verdra Beach, FL: Work Systems Associates. 1989)

CHAPTER 11

PULLING IT ALL TOGETHER
Becoming a Talent Optimizer

KEY ENABLERS

Leadership

Culture

THE TALENT MANAGEMENT SYSTEM

Strategic Alignment

Performance Management

HR Capability

Talent Assessment

Learning & Development

Talent Data Analytics

RESULTS

The Best Talent

Lower Cost

Improved Diversity of Talent

Improved Business Outcomes

Optimizing Talent, pages 139–148
Copyright © 2011 by Information Age Publishing
All rights of reproduction in any form reserved.

Having read our book, you can now see that each component of the Talent Optimization Framework™ (TOF) is connected to the others. For instance, if your business strategy changes, the other parts of model will be affected; if your leadership requirements change, the other elements must be refreshed.

The framework represents a method by which it is possible to continuously improve and keep your talent approaches fresh, current, and most importantly, beneficial to the organization. Used well, it becomes part of the operating rhythm of your company and a core competency of every leader. In this way, optimizing talent becomes embedded in your organization's DNA.

Consistency, continuous improvement, and clarity, combined with a regular process and methodology for implementation, are the keys to success. We offer this advice to those wanting to lead their organizations in becoming talent rich:

- Use the Talent Optimization Framework™ and Survey to get a picture of where you stand today relative to talent.
- Don't just take the survey yourself, but get others' opinions of how they see the world of talent. Get the views of line managers and employees and see if there are disconnects between your view and theirs.
- Facilitate a dialogue with your senior team to discuss the survey results, gain agreement on the collective view of talent, select key improvement areas, put a strategy and plan in place, and regularly monitor progress.
- Use the information from your talent plan in your regular business reviews. For example, when you are conducting reviews of your business strategy and operational plans, include a review of your talent strategy based upon the TOF in order to ensure alignment.
- Regularly check your pulse on how you are doing against your TOF plan. Track and measure improvement.
- Talk about progress in all your team meetings. Be transparent about where you are strong, what needs to be improved, and what you are doing about it.

While this advice may seem self-evident, we have seen many leaders start out with good intentions and then get distracted. Make this part of your regular business discipline. Making it part of your routine can ensure continuity and embed it into your organization's culture.

Are You a Talent Optimizer, Talent Neutralizer, or Talent Minimizer?

Now that you have read about each aspect of the Talent Optimization Framework™ and seen the compelling analysis for how it links to business success, it is time for you to get a view of where you stand as a talent optimizer. Use this quick quiz to gauge where you are on the talent optimization scale.

Use the following 3-point scale:
1 = No; not at all   **2** = Sometimes; but inconsistently   **3** = Yes; all the time

1. Do you consistently communicate the importance of talent development and growth to your team?
2. Do you seek out talent and help promote careers?
3. Do you encourage talent movement?
4. Do you teach courses on leadership skill development?
5. Do you "walk the talk" and operate consistently within your values?
6. Do you seek feedback on how you are doing personally?
7. Do you have a clear talent strategy that you regularly communicate?
8. Do you know the leadership characteristics required to successfully implement your business strategy?
9. Do you know the strengths and development needs of your direct reports?
10. Do you know the skill sets for the talent you need to hire in the future?
11. Do you use clear and consistent assessment techniques in evaluating your talent?
12. Do you regularly give feedback to your employees?
13. Is your feedback primarily focused on letting people know what they are doing well and how to leverage their skills in the future?
14. Do you consistently coach your employees?
15. Do you encourage your people to get development?
16. Do you think ahead and develop plans for the next roles of your team members?
17. Do you focus on your own development?
18. Do you partner with HR to develop talent solutions?
19. Do you use your HR leader as a coach?
20. Can you effectively measure the level of leadership quality on your team?

If you scored 3's on all answers or 60 points, you are a gold medal champion and role model for talent optimization.

If you scored more than 45 points you are a talent optimizer. You have some work to do to be a gold medal champion, but you are on the path to success.

If you scored 25 to 44 points, you are a talent neutralizer.

If you scored less than 25 points, you are a talent minimizer, and there is much work for you to do.

Figure 11.1   Talent Optimizer Quiz.

No matter how you scored on this test, get started with our talent optimizer tips and build yourself a plan for success.

Talent Optimizer Tips for All Leaders

Some of you may be saying, "I can't do this: my boss does not do this, and I can't if she is not supportive." We hear this argument frequently, but there are many things that you can do. Following are some quick and easy tips to becoming a talent optimizer. Whether you're a senior leader, manager, or a team leader, practicing these tips will put you on the path to success.

Leadership and Culture

- In every communication you make in staff meetings, in writing, or in presentations to your group, emphasize the importance of talent and employee development.
- Mentor two or three junior people in your organization and help them find their next best role when they are ready.
- Visibly reward development and those who coach and mentor others.
- Work on your own development and regularly ask for feedback from others. Get a coach for yourself.

Strategic Alignment

- Have specific talent goals for your group that are aligned to each of your specific business goals.
- Facilitate a session with your management team to discuss and agree on the talent strategy that supports and advances your business strategy or goals.
- Ensure everyone on your team and in your organization knows your talent strategy.

Talent Assessment

- Attend an assessment skills course and use the skills you learn regularly in your talent interactions and discussions.
- Use clear criteria and a rating scale when interviewing and selecting talent for hire or promotion.
- Don't allow anyone on your team to hire or promote someone on "gut feel." Be sure the leader can clearly state why this person is a good fit for the role and what his or her strengths and development needs are.

Performance Management

- Ensure that you know the career aspirations of your direct reports. Discuss career aspirations and skills needed to achieve the next career goal in all your performance dialogues.
- Make sure the learning goal from above is included in the performance plan and discussed in the reviews.
- Hold quarterly feedback sessions with each of your direct reports.

Learning and Development

- Teach a class about your favorite element of leadership.
- Take a course on coaching and pick one person to coach.
- Ensure that everyone in your group has one learning goal and that they are given time and support to achieve that goal.

HR Capability

- Use your HR person as a coach. Ask him or her for regular feedback on how you are doing as a leader.
- Conduct interviews jointly with HR.
- Use HR to facilitate discussions with your team around how to close the talent optimization gaps.
- Partner with HR in implementing your talent strategy.

Talent Data Analytics

- Pick two or three measures from your talent strategy and track the data around those measures.
- Conduct exit interviews and identify the reason(s) people are leaving.
- Conduct an employee satisfaction survey and track progress on improving scores.

Results

- Conduct the TOF Survey yearly and show improvements year to year.

While the list above is not meant to be exhaustive, these tips can serve as action steps to give you a quick jump start on your talent optimization journey.

Talent Optimizer Tips for Senior Executives

Senior executives have additional opportunities and responsibilities for ensuring that talent is a clear competitive advantage in their organizations. What follows are additional talent optimizer tips to assist senior leaders to get the best results from the TOF.

Leadership and Culture

- Promote talent and help rotate high-potential talent to new roles and opportunities.
- Promote an environment in which everyone is expected to learn from their mistakes and increase their skill sets.
- Conduct skip-level meetings with small groups (8–12) of leaders who are two levels below you in the organization; use these sessions to learn about the issues and ideas of the talent in the organization.
- Participate in the annual talent review process of the organization; make it a point to know the top 25% of emerging leaders in your organization.

Strategic Alignment

- For each strategic business goal that you have for your organization, identify the accompanying strategic talent goal that should be addressed to assure alignment.
- Create a spreadsheet with three column headings: 1) skills needed for today's business; 2) skills needed to compete in the future; and 3) talent gaps. Assess your leadership team based on these three criteria.
- Identify one to three development targets for your organization that align with the talent growth needed to win in the marketplace in the future.
- Publish a talent alignment document for your team that articulates how the talent of the organization needs to change and grow in order to fulfill the strategic vision of the organization.

Talent Assessment

- Conduct paired interviews and assessments with your leadership team to gain and give feedback regarding assessment skills.

- Hold team talent calibration sessions; use these sessions as an opportunity for your leadership team to discuss and provide evidence concerning the talent in the teams.

Performance Management

- Hold yourself accountable for having quarterly performance discussions with each member of your team; ensure that your managers are doing this with their teams as well.
- Establish clear and specific expectations for your managers regarding their role in the performance management process.
- In skip-level meetings with your up and coming leaders, ask for feedback on the quality and quantity of career discussions they have with their managers.

Learning and Development

- Identify special projects in your business that can be utilized to give select members of your organization an opportunity to stretch their skill sets while adding value to the business.
- Match up team members with opposite skill sets to work together on a project so that each gains exposure to the other's style and strengths.
- Support peer mentoring within your organization.
- Identify and track progress on the three highest priority development gaps in your organization.

HR Capability

- Partner with HR to develop job profiles for the key roles in your organization.
- Work with HR to develop organizational alignment around assessment, development, and performance management efforts.
- Use HR as your talent scout; continually look for high-potential employees who will be needed in the future.
- Invite HR to your staff meetings and to participate in your business strategy sessions.

Talent Data Analytics

- Analyze the impact of employee movement (new hires, promotions, transfers, exits) within your organization. Which way is the needle pointing regarding talent?

- Utilize team aggregate assessment data to better leverage group strengths and fill critical gaps.
- Use external benchmarking of top talent to raise the bar and identify talent needed to drive business results.
- Work with HR to establish an ROI for selecting and developing to the right competencies; demonstrate the relationship between behaviors and results.

Results

- Conduct the TOF survey yearly and show improvements year to year.

Talent Optimizer Tips for HR Professionals

We view the HR team as the leaders, teachers, partners, and facilitators of the TOF. If you are an HR person looking to help your business partners to improve their talent optimization, here are some quick tips to ensure this will happen.

Leadership and Culture

- Work with your leadership team to get a *simple* leadership framework with competencies (remember to keep it simple).
- Help your team members assess the culture and come up with a clear plan to address gaps.
- Learn the key elements of business strategy. Read a book or take a course on the subject.

Strategic Alignment

- Regularly participate in business reviews and attend the staff meetings of your business leaders.
- Meet customers and go on sales calls.
- Read the relevant trade journals; stay current on the issues impacting your company.
- Know how your business unit makes money or delivers on its goals.
- Understand how to read a balance sheet.

Talent Assessment

- Become an expert talent assessor. Take a course and then develop learning materials for your business unit. If you have HR professionals reporting to your team, make sure they are trained assessors as well.

- Create selection interview guides that are simple, user-friendly, and helpful to your leadership team to guide assessment discussions.
- Create a simple talent review process that uses assessment data to determine potential.

Performance Management

- Engage your business leadership team in a dialogue around how to conduct effective performance management. Help make it their process, not yours.
- Create a performance review process that is simple and captures accomplishments, strength and development needs, career aspirations, and potential next roles.
- Keep your process business friendly and train leaders in how to give effective and constructive feedback during reviews. Teach them how to have a development conversation.
- Keep the ratings simple, with good operational definitions, so everyone understands them.

Learning and Development

- Become an expert coach; earn a reputation for excellence in coaching your leaders.
- Develop career plans for your group, including specific learning goals.
- Help create one clear, simple, leadership competency model that anchors and aligns to all of your organization's development efforts.

HR Capability

- Brand the HR team as a strategic partner to the business
- Select, develop and certify HR team members to be experts in assessment, coaching, performance management and data analytics
- Create a 3–5 year HR strategic roadmap and identify the future HR capabilities required for "best in class" performance

Talent Data Analytics

- Learn how to construct and administer surveys to accurately collect data and how to conduct an organization diagnosis.

- Understand basic statistics and what questions to ask so you know what the data are telling you.
- Know what talent data are most important to business success and develop plans for collecting and analyzing these data points.

Results

- Learn how to show results using compelling data.
- Paint a picture of the organization with information and facts. Link this information to business outcomes.
- Regularly communicate the results openly and fairly on all talent processes in the group or business you support.

Human resources can play such a critical role in helping leaders become talent optimizers. This is your opportunity to continue to provide real value to the organization.

In closing, we would like to invite each of you to complete a full Talent Optimization Framework Survey™ for your organization. To do so, type the link below into your browser. Once you have completed the survey, we will provide you with a scorecard of your results, as well a comparison of how you match up to our best-in-class norms.

http://www.optimizingtalent.com/survey/

About the Authors

Dr. Linda D. Sharkey, PhD

Linda D. Sharkey is an HR executive and business strategist with extensive experience in Fortune 10 companies coaching, developing leaders and teams, and driving talent initiatives that support productivity and company growth. She is a founding member of the Marshall Goldsmith Group focused on helping successful executives become even more successful through executive assessment, coaching, and leadership development. Dr. Sharkey is also a Distinguished Fellow at the Global Leadership Development Center at Alliant International University.

Prior to joining the Marshal Goldsmith Group, Linda was VP of People Development for HP and held executive human resources positions at GE. At GE she designed a high impact leadership development initiative named a best practice by Jack Welch.

Linda is widely published in the area of leadership development, culture change, and executive coaching. She is frequently a keynote speaker at company events, Linkage, Talent Management Magazine conferences, Conference Board, and the Organization Development Network. Linda holds her PhD from Benedictine University in Lisle, Illinois, which is where she met her co-author. Linda and her husband Tom live in Saratoga, California.

Paul H. Eccher PhD

Paul H. Eccher possesses more than 20 years' experience in helping clients to leverage talent. He is expert in the areas of executive assessment, coaching for performance, and talent management audits and applications.

Optimizing Talent, pages 149–150
Copyright © 2011 by Information Age Publishing
149

Before founding The Vaya Group (formerly known as Corporate Insights, Inc.), Paul led a team of talented industrial psychologists who designed and implemented competency models and behaviorally based assessment systems to assist clients in their talent acquisition, alignment, and development processes. He has studied the characteristics and behaviors of top-performing leaders in well over 100 corporations, including Hewlett- Packard, General Electric, Northwestern Mutual Life, Campbell's Soup, Takeda Pharmaceuticals, Astra Zeneca, and McDonald's Corporation. In addition, he has coached and developed executives to bring about positive, behavioral change and improved leadership capabilities. He has assisted clients to understand the leadership competencies and talent management systems, which drive performance success within unique cultures. He has conducted numerous research studies linking work force capabilities to bottom-line measures of performance.

Paul received his PhD in Organization Development from Benedictine. His dissertation centered on the culture of leadership within a Fortune 10, multi-national corporation. He is a founding member of Benedictine University's Values-Driven Leadership Center.